THE GREAT

WEAPONS HERESY

Also by Thomas W. Wilson, Jr.

Cold War and Common Sense

THE GREAT
WEAPONS HERESY

Thomas W. Wilson, Jr.

Houghton Mifflin Company Boston

1970

The author is grateful for permission to quote
from the following sources: The Open Mind by
J. Robert Oppenheimer, copyright © 1955 by J.
Robert Oppenheimer, Simon and Schuster, Inc.;
Men and Decisions by Lewis L. Strauss, copyright
© 1962 by Lewis L. Strauss and the Lewis L.
Strauss Literary Trust, reprinted by permission of
Doubleday and Company, Inc.; "Atomic Weapons
and American Policy" by McGeorge Bundy, published in the July 1953 issue of Foreign Affairs,
copyright © 1953 Council on Foreign Relations,
Inc., New York, and "To Cap the Volcano" by
McGeorge Bundy, published in the October 1969
issue of Foreign Affairs, copyright © 1969 Council
on Foreign Relations, Inc., New York.

First Printing c

Library of Congress
Catalog Card Number: 70-82946

Printed in the United States of America

For

My Father

Acknowledgments

As everyone knows from "Acknowledgment" pages, no writer can finish a book without active or passive help from family and friends who, through no fault of their own, are doomed to share the ordeal vicariously. In the present case, I shall mention only my wife, who is not without responsibility: she talked me into reading the transcript of the Oppenheimer hearing in the first place. On second thought, my children and stepchildren provided a sort of stimulus with irreverent humor about the pace of progress on the enterprise.

The book has been written in bits and pieces, in fits and starts, and in four countries over a period of some five years. I shall certainly miss mentioning some of those who helped along the way, and to them I apologize in advance. But one who helped was Harriet Wilkins, who has an uncanny way of running down facts and wheedling documents away from reluctant librarians. I am grateful to her. I am thankful, too, to Tam Lutz, Paula Vezina, Mary Reordan, and Wanda Maltz, who typed chunks of the manuscript along the way. Bernadine Bocian did that and much more. Thanks.

I have no debts to acknowledge to participants in the "Oppenheimer case" as such; rightly or wrongly, I refrained deliberately from seeking them out. Nor did I, of course, draw upon any official documents that might have come to my attention.

The book will have to stand as my own interpretation of Oppenheimer's role as creator, critic, and heretic of the atomic age — and of our curent fix with respect to strategic nuclear weapons.

THE PROBLEM of doing justice to the implicit, the imponderable, and the unknown is of course not unique to politics. It is always with us in science, it is with us in the most trivial of personal affairs, and it is one of the great problems of writing and of all forms of art. The means by which it is solved is sometimes called style. It is style which complements affirmation with limitation and with humility; it is style which makes it possible to act effectively, but not absolutely; it is style which, in the domain of foreign policy, enables us to find a harmony between the pursuit of ends essential to us, and regard for the views, the sensibilities, the aspirations of those to whom the problem may appear in another light; it is style which is the deference that action pays to uncertainty; it is above all style through which power defers to reason.

J. Robert Oppenheimer

Contents

Introduction

CONTROVERSY about the case of the United States Government versus J. Robert Oppenheimer refuses to die; the literature continues to accumulate as the furor simmers for a while and then boils up again.

It began on June 29, 1954, when the United States Atomic Energy Commission announced officially that it had withdrawn clearance for access to classified data from Dr. Oppenheimer — theoretical physicist, renowned teacher, "father of the A-bomb," holder of the government's highest civilian award for national service, principal architect of the "Baruch Plan," former chairman of the General Advisory Committee of the Atomic Energy Commission, director of the Institute for Advanced Study at Princeton, New Jersey, frequent consultant to governmental agencies and their contractors on many of the most sensitive aspects of national security policy, and symbol of a restless new partnership between science and government.

It was clear at once that the government's action was not the product of panic or accident. It was a deliberate, determined affair. But this is about all that *was* clear; there were few answers to some basic questions.

The Atomic Energy Commission had resurrected charges of "associations" with Communists and fellow travelers in the 1930s and raised them against Oppenheimer in the 1950s. Yet those associations were recorded in immaculate detail in a dossier familiar for years to the FBI, the military counterintelligence services, the White House, and to various high officials of the government, including the commissioners of the AEC, who repeatedly had reviewed that record and cleared Oppenheimer for access to much of the most highly classified material in Washington. *Why?*

The AEC at first accused Oppenheimer of having advised against pursuit of the H-bomb when the advice in question was not only his but the unanimous opinion of a panel of seven scientific advisers. Having accused him of this, the commission later denied that his opinions entered into the case at all. *Why?*

The AEC took radically disruptive, formal action against Oppenheimer when it would have been a simple matter to bring his services to the commission quietly and informally to an end. *Why?*

The 997-page published transcript of Oppenheimer's hearing before a Personnel Security Board shed little light. The "findings" of the board, together with subsequent conclusions by the general manager of the AEC and by its five commissioners, only compounded the mystery: the documents are internally inconsistent, mutually contradictory and, in critical respects, at odds with the evidence in the transcript.[1]

If the issue was "loyalty" to the United States, Oppenheimer's loyalty was explicitly and unreservedly attested by the Personnel Security Board.

If the issue was the "security" of classified information, the board went out of its way to praise Oppenheimer's unusual discretion in safeguarding classified data.

If the issue was Oppenheimer's former "associations" with Communists and fellow travelers, the principal witnesses called by the AEC were neither qualified to testify on the point nor were they asked to.

If the issue was Oppenheimer's judgment about the desirability of developing the hydrogen bomb, the general manager of the AEC and the commissioners stoutly denied his judgments were in question.

If the issue was "character," an extraordinary parade of distinguished witnesses, in sworn testimony, offered effusive praise for the character of the accused.

A great deal was written initially about the Oppenheimer case by authors and journalists who relied heavily upon the evidence in the massive transcript of the hearing. Long articles, padded with excerpts from the testimony, appeared immediately after the hearing in the daily press and in the weekly news magazines. Joseph and Stewart Alsop weighed the evidence for *Harper's*; Arthur Schlesinger, Jr., did the same for *The Atlantic*; and, as time went on, other monthlies and quarterlies, here and abroad, addressed themselves to whatever angles of the affair intrigued their editors or authors.

By 1955, Charles P. Curtis produced a book, *The Oppenheimer Case,* which concluded in effect that the government's evidence would not stand up in a court of law. James Shepley and Clay Blair defended the action of the government in *Hydrogen Bomb: The Men, the Menace, the Mechanism.* Robert Jungk went into the case in *Brighter Than a Thousand Suns.* Lewis L. Straus recorded his version in *Men and*

Decisions, as did former President Eisenhower in his own memoirs; a number of books by nuclear scientists touch on the case; and in the years that followed, Haakon Chevalier wrote both a novel and a nonfictional account from his own rather special point of view.

Much has been published, too, about Oppenheimer's personal role in the dawn and predawn of the atomic age, especially his directorship of the Los Alamos laboratory — notably by Leslie B. Groves in *Now It Can Be Told* and later by Lansing Lamont in *Day of Trinity* — but also in other books and special-interest magazines like *Science* and *The Bulletin of the Atomic Scientists.*

Oppenheimer's part in preparing the Baruch Plan is revealed in greatest detail in the second volume of the *Journals* of David E. Lilienthal. His positions on the use of the first atomic bomb against Japan and on the decision to go from nuclear to thermonuclear weapons have been discussed — if not always accurately — in many published writings.

The Oppenheimer story also is imbedded in the larger chronicle of the end of the Second World War and the early postwar years. Here the documentation is too rich for citation; the memoirs or published papers of President Truman, Senator Vandenberg, and Secretaries Stimson, Forrestal, Stettinius, and Byrnes are among the sources. There are dangers here, then, of reworking familiar ground. These are compounded by distractions inherent in both the complexities of the story and in the dramatic and contentious character of many of the side issues.

For one thing, there is a powerful temptation to become overly fascinated with the personality, politics, and especially the intellect of an obviously extraordinary man. Much about

Oppenheimer's personal qualities can be found in the transcript of the hearing, most interestingly perhaps in the testimony of George Kennan; Oppenheimer's death in 1967 inspired published reminiscences and judgments including those of Hans Bethe; five scientists who knew him well have since gathered their thoughts about the man in a volume entitled *Oppenheimer*; and the play entitled *In the Matter of J. Robert Oppenheimer,* by Heinar Kipphardt, presents the author's version of Oppenheimer's inner struggles.

For another thing, it is easy to be sidetracked by the issues which involved Oppenheimer. An example is the decision to bomb Hiroshima and Nagasaki, explored in Henry L. Stimson and McGeorge Bundy's *On Active Service in Peace and War* and Robert J. C. Butow's *Japan's Decision to Surrender.* Another is the question of "guilt" among scientists and the differences within the scientific community itself, which have been examined at length in such books as *American Scientists and Nuclear Weapons Policy* by Robert Gilpin and *Lawrence and Oppenheimer* by Nuel Pharr Davis.

It is tempting, too, to be seduced by the mysterious facets of the Oppenheimer case, such as the "Chevalier incident" about which so much has been written though so little is actually known.

There is always a tendency, when faced with complexity, to take refuge in easy generalization as, for example, did *Life* magazine in blaming the case on "the climate of the times." [2]

Some writers have offered personal judgments about the outcome of the Oppenheimer case. The Alsops, for instance, found it "a shocking miscarriage of American justice." Others have identified to their own satisfaction Oppenheimer's principal antagonists. Still others — often straining hard at the evidence — see the story as a morality play, a Greek tragedy, or a conspiracy. There seems to be an angle for almost everyone, villains to suit most tastes, and outlets for many a political prejudice or ideological predilection.

Yet there has been no satisfactory answer to the first and pivotal question: Why did the United States Government single out a particular adviser — in this case the most prestigious of its consultants — and, at a particular time, drive him from government service?

Late in 1969 Philip M. Stern's *The Oppenheimer Case: Security on Trial* was published. In fascinating detail, based on prodigious research, Stern systematically exposes the Oppenheimer "security hearing" for the farce that it was. He projects the story into contemporary times by insisting that the "personnel security system" which was twisted almost beyond recognition in the Oppenheimer case is still being abused and should be abolished. Several chapters of this book deal with material carefully examined by Stern; our purposes in doing so, however, while not contradictory, are broadly different. Incidentally, Stern's collaborator, Harold Green, plans to produce yet another volume on the subject.

It is the contention of the present author that whether Robert Oppenheimer was a benevolent genius or an arrogant intellectual, or a bit of both, is irrelevant; that Hiroshima is quite another story; that the feuding among scientists was but a side event; that the "Chevalier incident" is a trivial bit of nonevidence; that "moral" issues were of no substantial influence; that McCarthyism could not possibly be the central motivation for the Oppenheimer case; that the undoubted abuse of the security system only deepens the mystery of this particular story; that it doesn't help at all to be appalled by the existence of nuclear weapons, or angry at the FBI, or hard or soft on Communism; and that an ideological approach to the Oppenheimer affair is guaranteed to come a cropper. Much of this will be disputed.

Yet the unexplained fact remains that the Atomic Energy Commission's Personnel Security Board formally, explicitly, and unanimously cleared Oppenheimer on charges of being a "security risk" in the ordinary meaning of the term, and then proceeded by majority vote to revoke his security clearance. The narrower but deeper question then becomes: in what *extraordinary* sense could the administration have believed that Oppenheimer's continued employment would somehow affect national security interests adversely? What did Oppenheimer say, or do, or stand for that led a group of men to conclude that he was in some way a danger to the national security as they understood it?

The principal difficulty in getting to the root of the affair lies in taking it seriously as a loyalty or a security case, and in assuming that the target was no more than a man named J. Robert Oppenheimer. It is clear that even some of the direct participants did just that. It also is clear that McCarthyism, abuse of the personnel security system, personal animosities, moral confusion, and Oppenheimer's own affronts to men of slower wit all played their parts as the case unfolded.

But with the closer examination made possible by perspective it is clear, too, that the "matter of J. Robert Oppenheimer" involved issues far deeper than any of these: for his was a story of a world imprisoned by political and military tradition made obsolete by the atomic bomb, the first technological product of a revolution in the science of physics. Oppenheimer participated in that revolution and presided over its first technological application. He also understood that the advent of the atomic age was in head-on conflict with the deepest traditions of the sovereign nation-state and the traditional ways in which nations sought national security in a hostile world. He harbored perceptions believed at the time to be extremely dangerous — and he was vulnerable.

Oppenheimer was much more than a technical adviser on atomic energy matters; he was in a position to influence national security policy. Surely the clue to the government's case against him must lie, then, in the discovery of some fundamental difference of opinion on security policy and military strategy — or something even more basic.

From this approach, the story of the U.S. Government versus J. Robert Oppenheimer assumes the epic proportions of the atomic age itself, its issues completely contemporary.

Robert Oppenheimer had a very special — almost unique — knowledge of nuclear weapons, weapons effects, and the nuclear arms race; he was addicted to rationality, to a distrust of secrecy, and to the habit of testing inherited assumptions; and he nourished an almost absolute faith in the virtues of the open society.

For some eight years after the birth of the atomic age Oppenheimer engaged in a long, agonized, and often lonely intellectual struggle to comprehend the impact of nuclear science upon the national security needs of the United States — to resist what he believed to be the corruption of democratic society by excessive official secrecy — and to assert the duty of the open mind to challenge the most hardened of the human conventions.

This struggle led Oppenheimer to speak out about the facts of nuclear life as he saw them. It led him to become an open, articulate critic of official military strategy. Eventually it led him into heretical prophecy about the long-term effect of the nuclear arms race on national security policy.

Oppenheimer was convinced that the atomic age called for a renunciation of obsolete political and military traditions. He believed that the course of the nuclear arms race would force a radical revision of the very way in which men *thought about* national security and international relations in the atomic age. What's more, he insisted that the secret issues should be debated publicly.

From a legal or administrative point of view, the "security risk" hearing in the matter of J. Robert Oppenheimer was an elaborate hoax; the government had something quite different in mind when it moved against Oppenheimer, something which had nothing at all to do with "loyalty," "associations," or "character." In one formulation, the issue was whether an open society could stand the shock of discovering it had become an unwilling but ironbound prisoner of the past; and the question still stands today.

Thus the "Oppenheimer story" continued beyond the death of its principal; indeed its real climax, in all probability, only began to unfold tentatively on November 17, 1969, when Soviet and American delegations held their first preliminary meeting in the Strategic Arms Limitation Talks.

The story must begin, though, with a few words about the

sinner; for as Saint Augustine wrote in the fifth century: "You are not to suppose, brethren, that heresies can be produced through any little souls. None save great men have been the authors of heresy."

THE GREAT
WEAPONS HERESY

1

Prodigy in a Golden Age

OPPENHEIMER had grown up in an atmosphere which fed his intellectual bias and creative bent. His father was a youthful immigrant from Germany who prospered quickly in the textile import business in New York. His mother was a painter and a former teacher of art from Baltimore. The Oppenheimers lived quietly and comfortably without financial worries, valued the world of the intellect and culture, collected French impressionist paintings, and looked to the education of their children — Robert and a second son named Frank.

From the earliest years of his life, it was evident that J. Robert Oppenheimer was no "little soul." Others have told stories of Oppenheimer as a precocious child with an ever-restless mind and uninhibited curiosity: how he harassed his preschool tutor with questions beyond the teacher's competence; how he read his first professional paper to the New York Mineralogical Club at the age of twelve — the society's only nonadult member; how he accumulated languages and delved into philosophy; how he lost himself in lonely bouts of intensive reading in one field of knowledge after the other — considering careers of poet, painter, or architect until, at Harvard, he was drawn first to chemistry, then to experimental physics, then to theoretical physics. Here Oppenheimer found not only a beauty in the order and harmony of nature but ferment and excitement as well.

In the first two decades of the twentieth century, the once quiet world of Newtonian physics was in an uproar. New theories, hypotheses, concepts, and discoveries challenged, among other things, the assured properties of the atom, long thought to be the ultimate and, by definition, indivisible unit of matter. The received doctrine was in disarray; the conventional wisdom was shattered; paradox was piled upon paradox; and more questions than answers came tumbling from the minds and laboratories of a handful of mathematicians, chemists, and physicists in Europe who were formulating the "New Physics."

There were three principal nurseries of atomic science. One was at the medieval college at Göttingen in Germany. The second was in Copenhagen, where Niels Bohr conducted his experiments, made his calculations, worked with a few graduate students, and served as a kind of guiding spirit of the quickening intellectual revolution. The third was perhaps the best physics laboratory in the world at the time — the Cavendish Laboratory at Cambridge University. It was presided over by the hulking New Zealand scientist, Ernest Rutherford, who was the first to transform an element of nitrogen into an element of oxygen or hydrogen.

In retrospect it seems almost inevitable that Robert Oppenheimer would be drawn to the centers of this ferment. After graduating in three years from Harvard, magna cum laude, he left Cambridge, Massachusetts, for Cambridge, England, to work with Rutherford. After a year there, Oppenheimer moved on to Göttingen to take a doctorate.[1]

In the late 1920s and early 1930s Göttingen was the epicenter of an intellectual earthquake — one of those sudden, brief, and inexplicable golden ages of creativity and discovery. Most of the physicists whose names have since become household words were there as students: Fermi, Dirac, Szilard, Teller, Von Neumann, Blackett, Gamow, Kapitza, Pauli, Compton, Wiener, and others. James Franck, Max Born, and David Hilpert led the faculty. Einstein came from Switzerland to lecture; the Curies came from Paris; Niels Bohr came from Copenhagen.

To the faculty and students at Göttingen in those days, this was the international world of science at its best. In that world, truth is the only goal, rationality the only method. The intellectual responsibility of the scientific mind is to challenge and test all doctrine, to expose all views, discuss all possibilities, and reject all errors in the free air of open debate. The process of discovery was imminent and endless.

This was the air that Oppenheimer breathed as a postgraduate student. It exhilarated him, and infected him for life. Writing of Oppenheimer after his death, Hans Bethe speculated that ". . . perhaps he wanted to perpetuate that feeling of continuous discovery which must have pervaded Göttingen. All through his life he was able to convey to all around him a sense of excitement in the quest of science." [2]

In any event, Robert Oppenheimer was in his element in the atmosphere at Göttingen. He was fluent in five languages and seemed to be at his best on his feet in extemporaneous discourse, spinning out abstract scientific speculations with dazzling excursions into the philosophical and metaphysical implications of the new discoveries and theories about matter and nature, and about man's relations to them. His was a gift that made friends and admirers — and surely bred resentment among some who found him perhaps a bit *too* articulate.

After Göttingen, Oppenheimer spent a year as a National Research Fellow at Harvard and at the California Institute of Technology: then he returned to Europe for another year at the University of Leiden — where he astonished everyone by lecturing in Dutch after his first few weeks in Holland. He also was a fellow of the International Education Board at Leiden. For another year he studied, taught, became a frequent contributor to learned journals — and decided upon a career as teacher.

At twenty-five, Oppenheimer decided to leave Europe, birthplace of the New Physics, and return to the United States to help plant the seeds of the new discipline. He accepted concurrent appointments as assistant professor at the California Institute of Technology at Pasadena and at the University of California at Berkeley, presumably intending to devote his life to the academic world.

2

An Opening to the Left

It is not a serious exaggeration to say that J. Robert Oppenheimer promptly became the leading teacher of a new generation of physics teachers in the United States. Hans Bethe puts it baldly: "J. Robert Oppenheimer did more than any other man to make American theoretical physics great." "His lectures," wrote Bethe, "were a great experience . . . In addition to a superb literary style, he brought to them a degree of sophistication in physics previously unknown in the United States. There was a man who obviously understood all the deep secrets of quantum mechanics and who yet made it clear that the most important questions were unanswered . . ." [1]

If Oppenheimer's reputation as a teacher spread through the academic world, his reputation as a kind of a Renaissance Man became a local legend at Berkeley. His erudition no doubt contributed to the awesome influence he had on his students. But, more than that, he seems to have exuded a kind of radiant spell which, when it occurs in politicians these days, is inevitably called "charisma."

Among his students and colleagues, admiration for Oppenheimer sometimes soared to the level of idolatry. Perhaps the most extreme case was a young professor of Romance languages at Berkeley, named Haakon Chevalier. Writing much later, Chevalier would recall that "the Oppenheimer I knew was brilliant, incisive, measured, resourceful, imaginative, challenging, always in command of the situation . . ." [2] Be that as it may, Oppenheimer seemed to do everything well — from his unending, restless intellectual pursuits to cooking or merely mixing martinis. And so people admired him lavishly — or resented him.

Much has been made of Oppenheimer's tendency to live in his own ivory tower in California, preoccupied with scientific, literary, and artistic abstractions — oblivious to the contemporary world about him. He was, however, far from a hermit; indeed he enjoyed company and was rather gregarious.

Though he followed closely the ongoing ferment in the New Physics, and continued to write for professional journals, several things were happening to him in the mid-to-late 1930s outside the realm of his science. For one thing, he fell in love with Katherine Harrison, wife of a professor at the University of California. She soon divorced her husband to marry Oppenheimer.

For another thing, he began to get interested for the first time in politics. His friends had much to do with this, but external events also opened his mind to the near and pragmatic world of politics and economics. It was an opening to the left.

There was no shortage of domestic "causes" in those days. The unemployed were marching on Washington, sit-down strikes were being waged in Detroit and company police had beaten up young labor organizers like Walter Reuther. Abroad, fanatical militarists had seized control of the Japanese government at pistol point — then invaded China in the name of a "Greater Asian Co-Prosperity Sphere"; Mussolini was trying to reestablish the Roman Empire by conquering, in the first instance, Ethiopia; in Germany, Hitler came to power preaching an amalgam of racism and violence; and in Spain an upstart Colonel Franco, with the support of a reactionary church and aristocracy and the active help of Mussolini's Fascists and Hitler's Nazis, led an insurrection against the recently formed Republican Government of Spain.

To some people the war in Spain looked like a dress rehearsal for a Second World War; and to some, ignoring the tyranny imposed by Lenin and compounded by Stalin, it seemed that the only bright spot on the whole bloody, dreary scene was the Soviet Union.

In the face of depression, fascism, and war, some Americans turned, at least briefly, to the Communist party. It seemed to offer the emotional consolation of a ready-made dogma with answers to the questions that perplexed them. Many more did not join the party but strung along with it.

Oppenheimer had friends, relatives, and colleagues in both groups. He was titillated by talk of Marxist ideals and by a "scientific" approach to the organization of society. But unlike some who adopted the gospel whole and raw, Oppenheimer took the occasion of a cross-continent train ride to read Karl Marx from beginning to end, and concluded that Marxism made little sense to him. He never embraced the Communist scriptures, though he agreed with some of the lessons.

Meantime the Japanese bombed Shanghai from the air,

Mussolini's son reported the glories of aerial bombs bursting "like beautiful flowers" on Ethiopian villages, and Franco perpetrated the horror of Guernica.

There was nothing historically new in the sacking of cities; but the airplane was doing something to war. And there was a theory behind it: it was called "strategic bombing." The principle was that the terror touched off by bombing a civilian population would lead to a complete breakdown of its social structure and thus to the destruction of the people's will to wage war — making it quite unnecessary to defeat the enemy's ground or naval forces. One of the earliest theoreticians of this new dimension of war was the Italian general Giulio Douhet, who propounded his theses shortly after the First World War. General Douhet soon had disciples — among them U.S. General Billy Mitchell.

In any event, in the mid-1930s Robert Oppenheimer signed up with Communist-front organizations in California and his name appeared on their letterheads. He helped organize a teachers' union. He read the *People's World*, a West Coast Communist newspaper. Above all, he attended rallies and fund-raising parties for Loyalist Spain; and he contributed regularly, sometimes through an official of the Communist party, to the various organizations set up to support the Spanish government and the refugees who preferred exile to life under Franco.

Yet before long things began to happen which made Oppenheimer uncomfortable about the simplistic faith of his left-wing friends. He could find no acceptable explanation for the great Stalinist purges of 1938. Along with others who had made common cause with the Communists and fellow travelers, Oppenheimer was shocked by Stalin's deal with Hitler in the spring of 1939. Dr. Charles Lauritsen, a professor of experimental physics at the California Institute of Technology, recalled in the course of the hearings a long discussion he had had with Oppenheimer about the so-called Molotov-Ribbentrop Non-Aggression Pact. They agreed, he said, on ". . . what a dangerous situation for the rest of the world, this combination of Russia and Germany could be," and became convinced that "this was the beginning of a war . . ." [3]

Bethe recalled on the same occasion Oppenheimer's distress at the fall of France in 1940. Oppenheimer, Bethe said, spoke of "how the fall of France meant an end to many things that he had considered precious" and how "it was very necessary to do something to save the values of western civilization." [4]

Even before the fall of France Oppenheimer was explicit about what he thought it was necessary to do. In the spring of 1940, he met his old fellow student from Göttingen, John von Neumann, who had left Europe to become a professor of mathematics at the Institute for Advanced Study at Princeton. During the Oppenheimer hearings Von Neumann testified: "What I do recall very clearly is that Dr. Oppenheimer was for intervention on the side of the western allies . . ." [5]

The United States, of course, did not intervene; but it would not be long before it would take on the job of serving as "the arsenal of democracy." Some of Oppenheimer's friends began to drift into defense work. Lauritsen, for example, went to Washington in 1940 to join the newly established National Defense Research Committee. Not long afterward he met Oppenheimer in Pasadena. On that occasion, according to Lauritsen, Oppenheimer asked "if I thought that there would be an opportunity perhaps later of his contributing to the work . . . Dr. Oppenheimer expressed the desire perhaps to join us . . ." [6]

But for the moment, it appeared, there was no great demand for theoretical physicists in war work.

3

Success in the Desert

A FEW YEARS after Oppenheimer left Göttingen, brown-shirted goon squads began to appear on the campus to hold rallies in the name of the Master Race and to beat up Jewish students. Within months of Hitler's seizure of power in 1933, seven Jewish members of the Göttingen faculty were informed without warning that they had been "retired." A Nazi political commissar soon arrived to supervise what was taught and not taught at Göttingen. One thing that was not taught thereafter was the theory of relativity; that had become, in Nazi Germany, "Jewish world bluff"; all that derived from Einstein and Bohr became "Jewish physics." All that was left was "German physics," whatever that was supposed to mean.

So the campus that had spawned a golden age of discovery in the first years of the New Physics became an intellectual wasteland in the first years of the Third Reich. One by one the Jewish physicists of Central Europe began to make their way out; in the end there was only one country with enough universities to absorb them.[1] And so, thanks

to Hitler, the world center of the natural sciences shifted
from Europe to America and laid the basis for a postwar
"brain drain"; thanks to Hitler, Leo Szilard and Enrico
Fermi came to share a basement laboratory at Columbia
University; thanks to Hitler three refugee Hungarians —
Teller, Von Neumann, and Szilard — got together to persuade Albert Einstein to send his famous letter to President
Roosevelt on August 2, 1939 — a month before Hitler invaded Poland — raising the possibility of a bomb using the
energy released from matter.

The Einstein letter was perhaps not as decisive as some
have thought in launching the United States on its quest for
an atomic weapon; but it foretold the oncoming day when
the frontiers of science would no longer be the exclusive preserve of academic theorists. Before long the United States
Government would be in urgent need of abstract thinkers
to man scientific laboratories which would become thence-
forth the nerve centers of the national defense establishment.
Robert Oppenheimer was one of them.

The story of the search for a way to release the energy
frozen in matter — of the hesitant beginnings that mush-
roomed into the Manhattan Project — of the sprouting of
huge secret installations at Oak Ridge and Hanford and Los
Alamos — of the mobilization of thousands of scientists and
engineers and the expenditure of $2 billion — of Fermi's
mastery of the chain reaction and other achievements, inventions, and discoveries — of the cooperation and contributions of the British and Canadians to the greatest research
and development enterprise of all time — of the awesome
birth of the Great Weapon at Alamogordo Flats: this has
been told and retold in a still-expanding shelf of records, ar-

ticles, and books. It is, of course, the story of how J. Robert
Oppenheimer, director of the secret weapons laboratory at
Los Alamos, came to be known as the father of the A-bomb.
Very little of it needs to be repeated here.[2]

Yet if the "security men" had had their way, Oppenheimer
might have remained free to devote himself to the academic
life. Like all entering upon government service, he had been
required to fill out a long questionnaire. After looking it
over, the officers in charge of security for the project did not
want to clear him because of his prior memberships in Communist-front organizations.

By this time, however, General Leslie B. Groves had become head of the atomic bomb project and he officially
ordered clearance "without delay, irrespective of the information which you have concerning Mr. Oppenheimer.
He is absolutely essential to the project." Indeed it was on
General Groves's recommendation that Oppenheimer later
was appointed director of Los Alamos. So in 1942 J. Robert
Oppenheimer left the academic world and became an employee of the United States Government, cleared for access
to secret data; and that was that — for the time being.

If General Groves took any risk in overlooking Oppenheimer's left-wing past, it was nothing compared to the gam-
ble of turning over to a theoretician, totally lacking in
executive experience, the immense administrative task of
planning, organizing, equipping, staffing, and directing what
became the world's greatest scientific laboratory. Yet Oppenheimer became overnight the inexhaustible administrator of an enterprise in which endless practical things had to
be accomplished — and all in a hurry. He seemed to be
everywhere at once — monitoring the work of the top sci-

entists, soothing their frustrations when it went badly, reviewing the problems, probing for new approaches. At the same time matters more mundane than scientific equations and engineering principles claimed the director's attention: crises and problems about roads and water and sewage and dust, about housing and schools and recreation and morale in a community, constructed in secrecy at forced draft, of some eight thousand people. He was coach, cheerleader, quarterback, troubleshooter, and father confessor rolled into one. The theoretical work was left mainly in the hands of his assistants.

One of Oppenheimer's most difficult roles at Los Alamos was that of buffer between the scientists and the military men who were their ultimate bosses, interpreting the needs of the scientists to the military and the needs of the military to the scientists. He was the middleman-broker in an extraordinary and often painful relationship.

Throughout this uneasy alliance the greatest source of friction stemmed from the "security" of the enterprise. In an effort to assure absolute secrecy, the Manhattan District insisted that work on atomic energy be "compartmentalized" so that none but a few people at the very top would know what the whole project was all about. It was a principle that flew in the face of scientific tradition. In the end, the Army simply could not make compartmentalization stick at Los Alamos. According to Bethe:

> One of the factors contributing to the success of the laboratory was its democratic organization . . .
> . . . everybody in the laboratory felt a part of the whole . . . Very often a problem . . . would intrigue a scientist in a completely different branch of the laboratory, and he would come up with an unexpected solution.

This free interchange of ideas was entirely contrary to the organization of the Manhattan District as a whole . . . Oppenheimer had to fight hard for free discussion among all qualified members of the laboratory . . .[3]

The environment could hardly have been more different; but the excitement, the expectancy, the quest for discovery were analogous to Oppenheimer's student days at Göttingen. And the evidence makes plain that for those who took part, the time spent at Los Alamos was the most memorable of their lives.

The need for security opened up a new, strange, and sometimes silly world — for scientists and soldiers alike. General Groves, in the course of the Oppenheimer hearing, said that in the entire span of his Army career he had never dealt with security matters until he became head of the Manhattan District and added: "The Army as a whole didn't deal with matters of security until after the atomic bomb burst on the world because it was the first time the Army really knew that there was such a thing, if you want to be perfectly frank about it."[4]

And John von Neumann testified on the same occasion about the "Buck Rogers universe" of military security:

. . . all of us in the war years . . . got suddenly in contact with a universe we had not known before. I mean this peculiar problem of security . . .

. . . We were all little children . . . None of us had been educated or conditioned to exist in this situation . . .

Oppenheimer existed uneasily in the new atmosphere of secrecy. On the one hand, he talked freely to security officers about his own past activities in the United Front. He accepted the need for stringent measures to protect the se-

crets of Los Alamos. And he often badgered the other scientists on behalf of the military about the importance of
security precautions, a need which many of them took very
lightly indeed, as General Groves would testify.

At the same time, Oppenheimer resented being put in the
role of informer against his old left-wing associates. He was
sometimes curt with investigators; on occasion he brushed
aside their questions as being irrelevant; once he declined to
give information about two former acquaintances on the
grounds that they were dead and could not defend themselves. And, in the early days at least, he tended to resolve
conflicts of loyalty on the basis of his own judgment.

It was just this tendency that led Oppenheimer into the
"Chevalier incident." The long and short of that over-
worked story is that Oppenheimer did not, at first, report a
comment made by his old friend Haakon Chevalier, which
could have been interpreted as an invitation to pass information on to the Russians; when he voluntarily reported it later
to security officers he refused to name the man who had approached him and invented a "cock-and-bull story" that
kept Chevalier's name out of it; and when General Groves
insisted he had to know, Oppenheimer identified Chevalier.

No more can ever really be established about the Chevalier incident than this; the "truth" — if it were ever known
— is lost forever; the implications can exist only in the im-
aginations of those who think it was important. What is
relevant is that ten years later it provided a handy weapon
for a broadside attack on Oppenheimer's "character."

But it is perfectly evident from secretly recorded interro-
gations made at the time that Oppenheimer was persuaded
in his own mind that Chevalier would not consciously be

guilty of abetting treason and that he therefore did not want to implicate him because "I know where I stand in these matters." And that's about the way it looked to the two officials most directly concerned at the time.

In the course of the hearing, Colonel John Lansdale, head security officer for the Manhattan Project, testified, "It was perfectly plain that Dr. Oppenheimer believed it was quite unnecessary to our security to know the names of the person or persons — the one who later turned out to be Chevalier . . . To my mind it was a sad exhibition of judgment, and an exhibition of ego that is quite unwarranted, but nevertheless quite common . . ." [6]

General Groves described his views of the Chevalier incident in these words: "I did know this: That he [Oppenheimer] was doing what he thought was essential which was to disclose to me the dangers of this particular attempt to enter the project . . ." Groves went on to say that Oppenheimer "was always under the influence of what I termed the typical American schoolboy attitude that there is something wicked about telling on a friend." [7]

In any event Oppenheimer did not have administrative responsibility for the security of the laboratory. That was the Army's job — a task which, as it turned out, was acquitted somewhat imperfectly.

The public records are full of accounts of what others thought of Oppenheimer's performance at Los Alamos: by his colleagues Edward Teller, Louis Alvarez, and many others; by his superiors, General Groves and Vannevar Bush and John J. McCloy; and by President Truman who, in awarding him the Order of Merit of the United States of America at a White House ceremony, read this citation:

For exceptionally meritorious conduct in the performance of outstanding service to the War Department, in brilliant accomplishments involving great responsibility and scientific distinction in connection with the development of the greatest military weapon of all time, the atomic bomb. As director of the atomic bomb project laboratory in New Mexico, his initiative and resourcefulness and his unswerving devotion to duty have contributed immeasurably to the successful attainment of the objective. Dr. Oppenheimer's accomplishments reflect great credit upon himself and upon the military service.

As the world knows, the end-product of Oppenheimer's labors at Los Alamos was put to the test on July 16, 1945, at 5:29:45 mountain time near Alamogordo, New Mexico, when an "atomic device" was detonated for the first time. As Oppenheimer described it later in an outrageous understatement, "It was a success."

The world knows, too, what followed that event: on August 7 an official telegram informed the leaders in Tokyo that "Hiroshima was destroyed by a single bomb"; on August 9 another telegram announced that "not a tombstone is left standing" in Nagasaki; on August 10, the Japanese offered to surrender provided only they could retain their Emperor; and on August 14 they accepted the condition that the Emperor would be subject to the control of the supreme allied commander. The Second World War was over.

Arguments about the manner in which World War II was brought to an end may persist until doomsday; that is another story. But the passage of time will not alter a central, documented point: Secretary of War Henry L. Stimson recommended to President Truman that the first two operational atomic bombs be used against Hiroshima and Nagasaki precisely because he hoped and expected that the psychological shock would induce the Emperor to break with rigid Japanese tradition and intervene personally in the affairs of state on the side of peace. And this is precisely what happened. After Nagasaki the Emperor went over the heads of the militarists still in control of the government, spoke directly to his people for the first time, and ordered them to lay down their arms. They did — and the planned American assault on the home islands of Japan was then canceled.

4

From Science to Politics

HISTORICAL REVISIONISTS and other polemicists have created a mythology about "good" scientists, morally opposed to the first use of nuclear weapons, and "bad" soldiers and politicians, who unleashed the terrors of the nuclear age on an innocent public.

Some of the scientists did, in fact, have moral qualms about the use of the weapon they had helped to create; and Oppenheimer was one of them. But for the most part such concerns were rooted in reasonably hard-headed security considerations — and in the predictable political dilemmas of the postwar world.

One of the first to express anxiety was Niels Bohr, who had escaped from occupied Denmark to England with the help of the British intelligence services, and who later accompanied a British team of scientists to Los Alamos. Bohr talked ceaselessly of the postwar implications of atomic energy to scientists at Los Alamos and Chicago; he even arranged to see Prime Minister Churchill and President Roosevelt to lay his concerns before them.

Bohr has been caricatured as the absentminded professor. But he saw at once the political realities of atomic arms in a postwar world in which "the nations united against aggression may face grave causes of disagreement due to conflicting attitudes towards social and economic problems." [1]

Bohr understood the radical dimensions of the alternative to a future nuclear arms race: a universal agreement with "far-reaching control measures" and "such concessions . . . as would hardly be conceivable unless all partners were assured of a compensating guarantee of common security . . ." He tended to ramble in his presentation but the core of his argument was this: To avoid an atomic arms race the leading nations of the world would have to forgo competition in favor of cooperation — substitute consent for coercion — subordinate the old concept of "national interest" to a search for common ground in international affairs — and adapt traditional doctrine on national sovereignty in the process. Nothing short of that would do once the war was over.

Oppenheimer talked with Bohr in the evenings at Los Alamos about the future of atomic energy, and he knew what Bohr had in mind. Writing of this later, Oppenheimer said:

> . . . He was clear that one could not have an effective control of atomic energy . . . and a free science and a free spirit of inquiry, without a very open world. He made this quite absolute . . . in principle everything that might be a threat to the security of the world would have to be open to the world.
>
> Bohr knew that the Communists took quite a disdainful attitude towards speaking or revealing the truth; he understood how very much this had gone beyond the tactical duplicity

recommended by Lenin to the most dangerous kind of self-delusion . . .

From all this he understood that it would not be quite in character for the Soviet Union to make an open world. He felt that it was essential to engage that government by a very early consultation—consultation in a hopefully cautious spirit of friendliness with an ally that had been invaded and occupied with a desperate defensive war. He hoped that we should be able to offer full cooperation in scientific progress . . . in a world in which there would be adequate safeguards and, above all, in an open world. He hoped that the situation in which the Russians would find themselves, and what we would have to offer them, and the opportunity for associating themselves with a great, forward-looking change in the world, might alter the whole character of Soviet policy, and thus set a new model of international relations . . .[2]

To Bohr the political alternatives of the postwar world were sharply defined — an open international community or an atomic arms race. He hoped to swap the secrets of the New Physics for a new society in Russia. He thought that it should be easier to agree not to produce weapons that no nation had in its arsenal than to give up weapons already in national inventories. He did not know then, of course, that the Soviets had begun work on a nuclear bomb in 1942 and that Stalin had his own atomic secrets.

In a memorandum to President Roosevelt, Bohr conceded the "difficulty and delicacy" of an initiative with the Russians and deferred to the "responsible statesmen who alone can have insight as to the actual political possibilities." But then he referred to the tradition of "world-wide scientific collaboration" and added: "personal connections between scientists of different nations might even offer a means of establishing preliminary and unofficial contact."

Bohr thought his interview with President Roosevelt had gone well; but after furnishing his subsequent memorandum, he had no further encouragement. Indeed, after comparing notes with Churchill, the President placed Bohr under special surveillance until the end of the war. The British and American leaders had gained the impression that Bohr wanted to turn over atomic secrets to the Russians at once. They might well have thought that agreement to "far-reaching control measures" based on the submergence of national sovereignty within a concept of "common security" was grotesquely irrelevant to Stalin's style of doing business. As it was they were having enough trouble dealing with Stalin on urgent questions about the conduct of a war in which they were allies.

Bohr was not alone in his concerns about the relevance of political and military tradition to the onrushing nuclear age. Oppenheimer wrote later that "Bush and Compton and Conant were clear that the only future they could envisage with hope was one in which the whole atomic development would be internationally controlled. Stimson understood this; he understood that it meant a very great change in human life . . ."

So did others, among them the signers of what became known as the Franck Report, written by a group of scientists at the Metallurgical Laboratory in Chicago, under the chairmanship of James Franck, formerly professor of physics at Göttingen, and then holding the same title at the University of Chicago. At one point the Franck Report said that ". . . the military advantages and the saving of American lives achieved by the sudden use of atomic bombs against Japan may be outweighed by the ensuing loss of confidence and by a wave of horror and revulsion sweeping over the rest of the world and perhaps even dividing public opinion at home." [3] This was the so-called moral argument against the first use of atomic weapons presented by the authors of the Franck Report.

The bulk of the Franck Report, however, advanced the practical argument that nuclear discoveries could not be kept secret, that an American monopoly could not be maintained, and that the United States, though first in the field of atomic weapons, would nevertheless be at a strategic disadvantage in a nuclear-armed world. There would be no defense, it stated, against the atom bomb. "In no other type of warfare does the advantage lie so heavily with the aggressor," and the United States could not consider itself protected against sudden attack merely by the "accumulation of a larger number of bigger and better atomic bombs." A nonaggressive state might have more bombs but would still live in greater peril than an aggressive state with lesser inventories of nuclear weapons.

Moreover, the United States would be uniquely vulnerable to nuclear weapons since the natural targets for atomic bombs are cities and the United States is the most urbanized of all large nations. "Russia and China," said the Franck Report, "are the only great nations at present which could survive a nuclear attack."

So the seven Chicago scientists agreed with Bohr that an urgent effort must be made to reach an agreement for international control of atomic energy before the first atomic weapon was used. The atomic age would bring political problems that could be resolved "only from the political organization of the world." Like Bohr, they concluded that "any international agreement on prevention of nuclear armaments must be backed by actual and efficient controls," because, as they put it, "no paper agreement can be sufficient since neither this nor any other nation can stake its whole existence on trust in other nations' signatures."

The authors of the Franck Report recognized the radical implications for national behavior and political tradition of the case that they were arguing. The achievement of an agreement to control atomic energy, they said, would "essentially depend on the integrity of intentions and a readiness to sacrifice the necessary fraction of one's sovereignty, by all the parties to the agreement." And like Bohr, the signers of the Franck Report left to others the job of devising a workable system of effective controls. This was a "difficult problem," they said, which "requires study by statesmen and international lawyers."

Bohr and the Chicago scientists understood that the old military and political tradition would be irreconcilable with the new atomic age. "Statesmen and international lawyers" would have to smash a lot of inherited crockery and banish a lot of received wisdom. Many an ideological tenet would go by the boards and many a closed place area made open before the world could adjust to Oppenheimer's success in the desert at Alamogordo.

That took the matter out of the realm of world science and thrust it smartly into the arena of world politics.

5

A Place to Start

During the difficult days at Los Alamos, Robert Oppenheimer, like most men caught up in intensive war work, dreamed and talked of getting back to the good old civilian life of prewar days. Like some of the others, he never quite made it.

Oppenheimer did, in fact, resign as director of Los Alamos and briefly return to teaching, but it was not much more than a gesture. Much of his time was spent traveling back and forth to Washington. He could not lecture to students on the West Coast and at the same time deliver testimony to Congress. Besides, he could not get away from the problems of what to do with the new power he had helped to release from nature. In retrospect it seems as inevitable that Oppenheimer would be drawn to Washington in the postdawn of the nuclear age, as it was for him to be drawn to Göttingen in its predawn.

When the Japanese surrender came, President Truman had been in office only a scant four months. He and his administration had to try to come to grips with the staggering fact

of nuclear power in an atmosphere of postwar jubilation —
with the need to convert surrender in Asia and armistice in
Europe into permanent settlements for peace — with domestic pressure to get the boys home at top speed — with demands to end rationing and price controls and hasten the return to "normalcy" — with enormous and novel tasks in the
administration of occupied ex-enemy territories, prostrate in
their ruins and saddled with millions of refugees — with
euphoria about the newborn United Nations — and with an
impending congressional election.

But for all the other pressures and turmoil, there was a
sharp sense of urgency in Washington about coming to grips
with the atomic age. On the day the first bomb was dropped
on Hiroshima, President Truman announced he would soon
make recommendations to Congress on how to control the
production and use of atomic energy within the United
States "and further recommendations . . . as to how atomic
power can become a powerful and forceful influence towards
the maintenance of world peace."

Three days later the President, in a broadcast report to the
nation about the just-completed Potsdam Conference, said,
"The atomic bomb is too dangerous to be loose in a lawless
world . . . until means have been found to control the
bomb . . . we must constitute ourselves trustees of this
force . . . to prevent its misuse, and to turn it into the chan-
nels of service to mankind. It is an awful responsibility . . ."

Less than five weeks after the formal Japanese suurrender
the President sent a special message to Congress requesting
immediate action on the control of atomic science on both
the domestic and international fronts; he said drastic and
far-reaching measures would be needed because:

. . . the discovery with which we are dealing includes forces of nature too dangerous to fit into any of our usual concepts . . . In international relations as in domestic affairs, the release of atomic energy constitutes a new force too revolutionary to consider in the framework of old ideas . . . The hope of civilization lies in international arrangements . . . The difficulties in working out such arrangements are great. The alternative . . . may be a desperate arms race which might well end in disaster . . .

During the first ninety days of the first year of the atomic age the central theme which ran consistently through official U.S. statements, messages, speeches, and declarations about nuclear energy was to the effect that the problem in the end was not a technical one in physics or public administration but a political problem in international relations: How does nation live with nation in the nuclear age?

This was, to all intents and purposes, what Niels Bohr had said in 1944, what the atomic scientists at Chicago had said in the following year, what the Interim Committee on Atomic Energy had advised the Secretary of War, what the Secretary of War had advised President Roosevelt and President Truman before the secret of Los Alamos had been revealed to the world at large, and what the Senate Special Committee on Atomic Energy would conclude after five months of hearings and study. They were all agreed on one thing: something revolutionary had happened which could not be absorbed by political and military tradition.

The British and Canadian partners in the wartime project were of the same mind. In November, Prime Minister Atlee of the United Kingdom and Prime Minister King of Canada came to Washington to discuss with President Truman a common policy on nuclear energy and how to lay the problem of international control before the world at large. After five days, the three heads of state issued an agreed declaration in which they concluded that the best and perhaps the only chance of internationalizing atomic energy lay with the United Nations. They were clear from the start that a trinity of issues was involved: control of atomic energy, East-West relations, and the relevance of the UN Charter to the postwar world.

A scant three months had passed since Nagasaki; the UN Charter had just been ratified by the Soviet Union and the first session of the United Nations General Assembly was scheduled for January 1946. At a meeting of the foreign ministers of the Big Three, which began in Moscow in mid-December, the Soviets, after offering a few amendments to a British-American draft, agreed to cosponsor a resolution calling for the establishment of a United Nations Atomic Energy Commission to devise a plan for international control of the uses of atomic power. When Secretary of State James Byrnes returned from the three-power conference at the end of December, he reported to the American public on the Moscow meeting. Among other things he said: ". . . at the root of the whole matter lies the problem of providing the necessary safeguards." It would be at the root of the matter for a long time to come.

Until that time not much thought had been given, in or out of government, to just exactly what was meant by "safeguards" or "international control" or an "inspection system." Neither Bohr, nor the authors of the Franck Report, nor anyone else had offered much in the way of concrete steps, for there were no precedents in international tradition for anything like this.

Soon the search for answers began. Secretary Byrnes appointed, under the chairmanship of Undersecretary Dean Acheson, a Secretary of State's committee composed of John J. McCloy, former Assistant Secretary of War, and the three men who supervised and directed the development of atomic energy: Dr. Bush, Dr. Conant, and General Groves. The crux of the committee's mandate was ". . . to study the subject of controls and safeguards necessary to protect this Government so that the persons hereafter selected to represent the United States on the [United Nations] Commission can have the benefit of the study."

The secretary's committee met promptly — and promptly appointed a board of consultants composed of David E. Lilienthal, then chairman of the Tennessee Valley Authority, who would serve as chairman; Chester I. Barnard, president of the New Jersey Telephone Company; Dr. Charles Allen Thomas, vice president and technical director of the Monsanto Chemical Company; Harry A. Winner, vice president in charge of engineering policy of the General Electric Company; and J. Robert Oppenheimer. The board of consultants became, in effect, a full-time working subcommittee of the parent group; the "committee" and "board" together became known as the Acheson-Lilienthal Committee.

This was the effective end of Oppenheimer's dream of returning to academic life; it was the beginning, too, of a new venture into the unknown, of a search for new methods of thought, not about physics but about how great nations deal with each other. On the domestic front, tradition could be swept aside. A radical solution could be — and was — imposed: a total governmental control over raw materials, research, development and uses of atomic energy. This was enacted into law when President Truman signed the Atomic Energy Act which was described at the time as the most revolutionary act ever passed by Congress. But the Acheson-Lilienthal Committee began work precisely at the point where the nuclear age came into head-on conflict with *international* tradition. And that was something which could be swept aside only by international agreement and control.

Lilienthal insisted from the start that the board of consultants have access to all "the facts" about atomic energy. And after the first technical briefing, he wrote in his journal:

> No fairy tale . . . no spy mystery, no "horror" story, can remotely compare with the scientific recital I listened to for six or seven hours today. I heard more of the complete story of the atomic bomb . . . than any but a few men have yet heard . . . [of] the utter simplicity and yet fantastic complexity of the peering into the laws of nature that is the essence of this utterly bizarre and, literally, incredible business . . .
>
> We are going to know the facts about this whole business . . . When that happens, we may get some insight into the very grave difficulty involved in building some kind of hope for the future . . . This is a fearful responsibility . . .[1]

A bit farther on he noted: "This is a soul-stirring experience . . . I feel that I have been admitted . . . behind the scenes in the most awful and inspiring drama since some primitive man looked for the very first time upon fire."

For the first weeks of its work, members of the panel read documents, held discussions, visited facilities — and listened to Oppenheimer, chalk in hand at a blackboard in front of the room, lecture about nuclear physics to a class of four quite adult students. The members appeared to be a disparate lot, and they were far apart in their initial approaches to the question as posed by Lilienthal: "Can a way be found, a feasible, workable way, to safeguard the world against the atomic bomb?" They agreed that they would not try to seek a single answer or even a preferred one; they would examine alternatives, analyze the advantages and disadvantages of each, and submit these alternatives to the Acheson committee as worthy of further study

Lilienthal drew upon his experience as administrative head of the Tennessee Valley Authority and began harping on a favorite theme of his. He had defended the administrative independence of the TVA with the argument that the United States as a whole is not a "manageable unit" for natural resource development, and he urged his colleagues to try to identify pieces of the problem of international control of atomic energy which might be of "manageable proportions."

Yet the more they looked at it, the more unmanageable the whole thing seemed. They studied requirements for an inspection team to keep an eye on a single reactor at Oak Ridge. With the number and size of reactors around the world bound to grow by leaps and bounds, the inspection teams began to look like armies. Indeed the whole idea of "inspection" seemed to come apart in their hands. It was not just a matter of the number of inspectors, but the qualifications they would need to insure against cheating a control system. Nuclear science was in its infancy; the technology surely would change rapidly. For an inspector to understand what it was he was inspecting, he therefore would need to be on the frontiers of knowledge about nuclear science.

After thinking it through, the board of consultants came to the conclusion that to place the national directors of im-

portant facilities on national territory under permanent suspicion of evasion of an international agreement — to subject
them to necessarily constant inspection by necessarily large
groups of "foreigners" — to interrogate scientists and some
categories of engineers and probe into hitherto guarded "industrial secrets" would do more to arouse suspicion and ani-
mosity among nations than to reassure them of their security.
And such a system, the board surmised, would be "as obnox-
ious to Americans as to others." [2]

After several weeks of gloomy deliberation and fruitless
study, the members of the board were thoroughly depressed.
They found themselves up against what looked like a blank
wall: the only system of security which held any hope in the
atomic age began to look like a cruel illusion. Lilienthal decided that the consultants should take a recess. In the interim he asked Oppenheimer to prepare an analysis of just
where they were in their search for fulfillment of their "fearful responsibility."

Meanwhile, the United Nations General Assembly had met
for the first time. A resolution authorizing establishment
of a UN Atomic Energy Commission, sponsored by the five
Permanent Members of the Security Council and Canada,
was approved as the Acheson-Lilienthal Committee was
holding its first meeting in Washington. The problem of
controlling atomic energy was thus in the hands of the
United Nations or, more precisely, in the hands of the major
powers in their roles as UN members. The question was:
Did the major powers want to control atomic energy on a cooperative basis?

The answer seemed to be coming all too forebodingly —
in deeds and words. Four months had passed since V-J Day;

seven months since V-E Day. And while other allies disarmed with all the haste they could muster, Soviet armed forces remained fully mobilized. The Red Army stayed on in eastern and central Europe. There were no signs of the free elections promised at Yalta, no progress at all toward a peace settlement, no agreement on reparations. Germany was divided and so was Berlin — inside the Russian zone of occupation.

In the fall of 1945, Stalin told a British journalist: "I do not believe the atomic bomb to be so serious a force as certain politicians are inclined to consider it. The atomic bombs are intended to frighten the weak-nerved, but they cannot determine the outcome of war since atomic bombs are by no means sufficient for this purpose . . . monopolistic possession of the atomic bomb cannot last long . . ." [3]

Five months later, after the Soviet Union had agreed with the United States and the United Kingdom to seek international control of atomic energy Stalin said in a public speech ". . . The First World War was the result of the first crisis of the capitalist system of world economy and the Second World War was the result of a second crisis." Then, after making it plain that the Soviet Union would continue to rely exclusively upon its own national muscle, Stalin made a chilling statement for those who were looking toward internationalizing the atom: "I have no doubt that if we render the necessary assistance to our scientists they will be able not only to overtake but also in the very near future to surpass the achievements outside the boundaries of our country." [4]

Oppenheimer later said of this period: "I have seldom been so gloomy in my life." But gloomy or not, he remained in Washington after the board of consultants began its recess, preparing the memorandum Lilienthal had requested. Their work seemed to be leading nowhere; they had reached a stage comparable to the "paralyzing crises" that arose in the work at Los Alamos. It was a time to draw back and to rethink, restudy, reexamine the assumptions and hypotheses.

This process led Oppenheimer to two new perceptions. First, the technical steps in the long and complex process of atomic energy development could be divided into "dangerous" and "safe" categories. To maintain airtight control over the dangerous stages at which materials could be diverted to weapons production would be far from child's play, but it was administratively conceivable — quite possibly within Lilienthal's conception of a manageable job.

Yet even when radically reduced in scope, the fundamental objections to a still very large inspection system remained: it would be negative, restrictive, and coercive — a police function however one looked at it — as long as the basic motivation was national rivalry. This still seemed to Oppenheimer to be a fatal flaw in the whole approach to control and inspection.

Up to that point, all thinking, writing, and discussion of nuclear controls had begun with the weapons end of the problem, with the urgent need to prevent the use of nuclear products for destructive purposes. Oppenheimer backed away and probed for a different avenue of approach. Suppose one started not in response to fear but in response to challenge — not with a view to policing action but with a view to stimulating action? That would lead in the direction of an international project to develop nuclear science for the benefit of everyone. And that would throw the problem of inspection and control into a wholly new context. Oppenheimer began to work out the new approach.

Development implies research. An international atomic

energy development agency would have to be deeply and creatively engaged in atomic science. If the international agency were itself engaged in research and development, then it would be on the frontiers of the new science; it would thus attract rather than repel leading scientists from all over the world. An agency engaged in developing the beneficial possibilities of atomic energy would encourage the growth of fundamental knowledge, "stirring the constructive and imaginative impulses of men rather than merely concentrating on the defensive and negative." [5] Such an agency could establish a monopoly over work at the dangerous stages but leave nations free to pursue their own national programs of safe activities if they chose to do so. And a nuclear energy development agency might establish "new patterns of cooperative effort" and begin to lead the way toward "the gradual achievement of a greater degree of community among the peoples of the world." [6]

Oppenheimer wrote a memorandum for Lilienthal and the board of consultants setting forth his new thoughts. When the group reassembled, the members were soon caught up in a new mood of hope and excitement. They thought they might have an answer. They soon abandoned the original idea that they could only come up with a range of alternative suggestions. On the evening of February 25 — just about a month after the work began — Lilienthal recorded in his journal:

> I am very happy tonight. We have developed a really original, distinctive, and I think completely sound idea as the theme of our recommendation on the atomic bomb. After weeks of sweating blood, of weary hours when we went every which way, we now have arrived . . . When everyone instantly

accepted as his own a completely new set of words to describe what we were after — security through cooperative development — as a substitute for the term "control," which has been habitual in every preceding discussion not only of our group but in all the official dissertations on the subject — I knew that we had made great headway . . .

Yet it was still rough going for the panel of consultants. Soon after recording the "great headway," Lilienthal noted in his journal:

It would be quite wrong if I did not record how weary I have been (tomorrow will be the third Sunday in a row I have worked) and how often there have been periods of almost unimaginable gloom. The gloom has come not only when we hit a serious snag, or can't seem to keep on the beam, but from the terrible realities of the bomb . . . I can't make clear how this hangs over everything . . .

The "terrible realities of the bomb" which hung over Lilienthal's labors were given extra dimensions by Dr. Teller, testifying before a congressional committee at the very time the board of consultants was stuggling for ways to contain the destructive force already available in atomic weapons.

"The atomic bomb is in its earliest infancy," Dr. Teller told the committee. "I am convinced that it will not be very difficult to construct atomic bombs that will dwarf the Hiroshima bomb in the same way that the Hiroshima bomb has dwarfed conventional explosives." What he had in mind, of course, was a thermonuclear, or hydrogen, bomb known to the scientists trying to develop it as the Super.

For all the agony of the Lilienthal panel, there was something of the excitement that Oppenheimer had known at Göttingen and Los Alamos — the sense of intellectual struggle with unprecedented problems, of great pressure and great urgency, of the search for innovations to take the place of worn-out tradition. Years later, Oppenheimer objected to the impression that he had been what he called the "big cheese" in the Acheson-Lilienthal group; as in the case of Los Alamos, he contended that the end product was the result of a team effort. But he did admit to having written about half of the Acheson-Lilienthal report; and something more than that proportion bears the mark of his prose style:

> We have concluded our deliberations on this most difficult problem, not in a spirit of hopelessness and despair, but with a measure of confidence. It is our conviction that a satisfactory plan can be developed, and that what we have recommended can form the foundation of such a plan.

The board predicted that its recommendations might meet with skepticism. "It did among us," the members said, "but thought and discussion have converted us."

The plan would raise inevitable doubts, they said. But they went on: "One should ask himself 'what are the alternatives?' We have and we find no tolerable answer."

When the board's report was presented to the senior committee, Dean Acheson, never known for careless compliments or casual bouquets, put it down and said simply, "This is a brilliant and profound document." President Truman called it a "great state paper." It would soon become known, with some minor amendments, as the Baruch Plan. And the consultants described it "not as a final place, but a place to begin . . ."

Whatever else may be said about it, the Acheson-Lilienthal report offered a radical political response to a radical breakthrough in science — and a substitute for threadbare tradition in interstate relations.

6

Failure at Lake Success

We are here to make a choice," said Bernard Baruch, "between the quick and the dead. That is our business." [1]

Mr. Baruch was making his first statement as chief United States delegate to the United Nations Atomic Energy Commission at its first meeting on June 14, 1946. In retrospect his opening formulation may appear a bit overblown; but it was a fairly accurate reflection of the mood and motivation of the United States Government as it prepared and then presented to the world at large the Baruch Plan for taming a force "too dangerous to fit into any of our usual concepts."

Just how radical the Baruch Plan was emerged for all to see as the United States, during the first month of proceedings at the UN, added flesh to the skeleton of policy and principle. In a memorandum for discussion in the commission the United States said that the new world authority should, among other things, ". . . obtain and maintain complete and exclusive control or ownership of all uranium, thorium, and other material which may be a source of atomic energy . . . acquire, construct, own and exclusively operate all facilities for the production of U-235, plutonium, and such other fissionable materials as may be specified . . . have unhindered access to, and power to control, license, and inspect all other facilities which possess, utilize or produce materials which are a source of atomic energy . . . have the exclusive right of research in the field of atomic explosives . . . foster and promote the non-dangerous use and wide distribution of atomic energy for beneficial purposes . . ." [2]

The proposed UN Atomic Development Authority would own nuclear facilities in many countries; it would produce and sell energy; national nuclear power facilities could operate only under UN license and with active materials leased for limited and specific purposes from the monopoly; national government agencies in the atomic field would, to the necessary extent, be subordinate to the world authority; officers and employees of the international agency would need guarantees of freedom of movement and communications to and from its far-flung facilities. John M. Hancock, a member of the United States delegation, summed it up in addressing the Institute of the National Committee on Atomic Information:

> . . . the Atomic Development Authority must have broad administrative powers. It will carry out policy. It will have to make important decisions, and actively operate a large-scale program. It must act. It could not operate if it had to secure unanimous approval of its action from any other organization. The Authority must have power — unequivocal, effective power — commensurate with its responsibilities . . .

The United States was prepared to give up its atomic monopoly; willing to forgo the pursuit of supremacy in the most modern of all weapons; ready to accept the binding authority of an international monopoly; offering to trade secrecy for openness and national competition for international cooperation in atomic affairs; and hoping to set a drastically new pattern of interstate relations for the nuclear age, provided only that others were willing to do the same. Niels Bohr could have asked for no more.

Meanwhile, Robert Oppenheimer was still caught up in the consequences of his success in the desert the year before; after some reluctance, he yielded to Baruch's appeals to join him in New York as consultant to the U.S. delegation to the UN Atomic Energy Commission. He soon became active with the Scientific and Technical Committee — one of the subgroups set up to assist the commission. The question put to the Scientific and Technical Committee was "whether effective control of atomic energy is possible." The committee was made up of scientists from each of the nations represented on the commission.[3] It was hoped that if scientists could get together and discuss feasibility on the technical level, without the intrusion of political distractions, agreement might be easier to reach. This was an echo of Bohr's hope that the universality of science, and the dedication of scientists to objectivity and rationality, might lead the way around political obstacles.

In many ways, the eighteen meetings of the Scientific and Technical Committee were, for Oppenheimer, a replay of his experience with the Acheson-Lilienthal Committee. The members agreed to begin with a systematic examination of "the facts"; to break down the problem into "manageable" parts; to meet informally in free exchanges unstructured by formal governmental positions; and to stop short of the political implications of their findings.

Under these conditions, the scientists arrived at an agreed report. Like the Acheson-Lilienthal report, it examined the various stages in the atomic energy process and identified the points at which controls would have to be established to prevent the diversion of fissionable materials to weapons use — that is, the "dangerous" stages. In the end the scientists concluded:

> With regard to the question "whether effective control of atomic energy is possible," we do not find any basis in the available scientific facts for supposing that effective control is not technologically feasible. Political feasibility is not discussed or implied in this report . . .

This was the first agreed report to emerge from the commission; it also was the last. On the political level, things went less well — though in due course and after some amendments, ten of the twelve members of the commission supported the U.S. proposals. The opposing members were Poland and the Soviet Union.

Ambassador Gromyko, who represented the Soviet Union, did not at first comment directly on the Baruch Plan. He presented, presumably as an opening gambit, a set of Soviet proposals which boiled down to this: first, all nations should exchange all their information about atomic energy; then all nations should stop manufacturing atomic weapons and destroy whatever such weapons they have; finally after these steps have been taken, a system of international controls could be worked out in subsequent negotiations.

As the debate went on, Gromyko, occasionally spelled by

the Polish delegate, began to say what his government thought
of the Baruch Plan: The American proposals were hatched
by "Wall Street monopolists"; the American intent was to
establish "imperialist control" over struggling and peace-
loving nations; the American version of an inspection system was a scheme to infiltrate "espionage agents" into other
countries.

Gromyko rang every change on these themes — and then
rang them again. Yet the beginning and end of the substantive Soviet position on the control of atomic energy
rested on another point which would be the substance of
all subsequent Soviet positions on any other arms control or
disarmament proposal for at least the next two decades:

> . . . The principle of sovereignty of States Members of the
> United Nations is one of the cornerstones on which the struc-
> ture of the United Nations is based. Violation of this principle
> would have far-reaching and negative consequences, not only
> for the activities of the United Nations Organization, but
> maybe for its very existence . . . we cannot accept any pro-
> posal which would undermine in any degree the principle of
> unanimity of the Permanent Members of the Security Council
> on all questions relating to the maintenance of peace and
> security.

In his opening speech, Baruch had said,

> . . . It might as well be admitted, here and now, that the
> subject goes straight to the veto power contained in the Charter
> of the United Nations so far as it relates to the field of atomic
> energy . . . There must be no veto to protect those who
> violate their solemn agreements not to develop or use atomic
> energy for destructive purposes.

When he read the Acheson-Lilienthal report, Rexford Guy Tugwell, former Governor of Puerto Rico and then a professor of political science at the University of Chicago, found in it "a revolutionary modification of attitudes toward national sovereignty."

Baruch, in speaking for the U.S. Government in the course of the debate at the UN, put it somewhat differently:

> Every treaty involves some diminution of absolute national sovereignty, but nations enter into such treaties of their own free will and to their common advantage. Indeed, freedom to enter into such voluntary international agreements is inherent in the concept of national sovereignty.

The Soviet Union, however, was not prepared to accept any diminution of absolute national sovereignty, even by voluntary international agreement. As other delegations pressed him, it became clear that by "international controls" Gromyko meant that each nation would "inspect" itself; that any suspected violation of agreements would be taken up in the Security Council; and that the veto power of the Permanent Members of the Security Council would remain inviolate.

Of course, Gromyko was right about the Charter of the United Nations: the principle of sovereignty for the member states was indeed written into it, and doubly insured for the Permanent Members by a veto on actions by the Security Council. So by the time of the first meeting of the General Assembly, the shiny new Charter of the United Nations already was obsolete as a framework for an international authority which Mr. Hancock had said "must have power — unequivocal, effective power — commensurate with its responsibility" to exercise "broad administrative powers," to "carry out policy," to "make important decisions," and to "actively operate a large-scale program." To this critical extent, the charter was a pre–atomic age document.

When the commission was about five weeks old, Gromyko wound up a speech with this: "In conclusion, I should like to say that the American proposals, as they are presented now, cannot be accepted by the Soviet Union either as a whole or in their separate parts."

The conclusion had been implicit in the first Soviet presentation. But the words came as a rough shock to many who had pinned high hopes on peace through international control of atomic energy. Lord Bertrand Russell was so upset that he became the first known public advocate of a preventive war against Russia — or at least the first proponent of nuclear blackmail; he proposed an ultimatum calling upon the Soviet Union to accept the Baruch Plan or face atomic bombardment. As he said later in a letter written on May 5, 1948, and subsequently published in the October 16, 1954, *Saturday Review:*

> . . . As soon as Russia rejected the Baruch proposals I urged that all nations favoring international control of atomic energy should form an alliance and threaten Russia with war unless Russia agreed to come in and permit inspection . . .
>
> There are some things of which Europeans are more vividly conscious than Americans. If Russia overruns Western Europe, the destruction will be such as no subsequent reconquest can undo. Practically the whole educated population will be sent to labor camps in Northeast Siberia or on the shores of the White Sea, where most will die of hardships and the survivors will be turned into animals, (Cf. what happened to Polish intellectuals) . . . I have no doubt that America would win

in the end, but unless Western Europe can be preserved from invasion, it will be lost to civilization for centuries.

Even at such a price, I think war would be worthwhile. Communism must be wiped out, and world government must be established . . .

World government was not in the cards; meanwhile Russell's views on how to handle the Russians did not appeal very strongly to governments. Instead of forming an alliance for nuclear war against the Soviet Union, they continued the talks at the United Nations.

As the weeks wore on, the debate in the Atomic Energy Commission acquired an air of the never-never land. On the last day of July, Lilienthal listened to the proceedings at the United Nations and the next day recorded this in his journal: "The whole thing didn't seem real. It seemed definitely *unreal* . . ." As it turned out, the proceedings of the United Nations Atomic Energy Commission would drag on for more than two years. They were fated to frustration, futility, and finally to boredom before dying out with a whimper.

The first major political act of the nuclear age was the U.S. decision to drop the bomb on Hiroshima, and the second was the Japanese decision to surrender after Nagasaki; the third and fourth major political acts of the nuclear age were the U.S. decision to offer the Baruch Plan and the Soviet decision to reject it. Why did they do it? In czarist Russia, suspicion of foreigners was endemic, secrecy was a way of life, and a very large military establishment was maintained in support of Russian ambitions abroad.

In revolutionary Russia, every leader from Lenin onward plowed scarce resources into the largest and most effective military forces they could afford at great sacrifice of other needs; with a domestic system based on force, Communist leaders could hardly imagine the pursuit of foreign objectives on any basis but force; and in all of Marxism-Leninism there is nothing to sanction cooperative arrangements based on consent among the nations.

Yet there was even more to it than that. In Moscow there was a fixed view of the nation-state and of how such states deal with each other. Nation-states, and particularly major powers, have "national interests" which by definition are conflicting; and the national interests of one major state can be advanced only at the direct and equivalent loss to the national interest of another. Thus, diplomacy in support of national interests is a tug-of-war game in which an inch gained on one side is an inch lost by the other — a struggle in which there are winners and losers but no common ground. To backstop the diplomatic game in support of the national interest, national security is defended by national armaments which in turn is a competitive enterprise: for superiority in arms is the obvious way to secure the safety of the state in a world where politics is characterized by the clash of conflicting interests of nation-states.

It was a very conventional and bourgeois view of international relations, a doctrine widely shared by philosophers, statesmen, and strategists of the nineteenth century. It gave rise to a geopolitical analysis of international affairs which largely guided the policies of the major European powers. Treaties were made, armed forces were deployed, a "balance of power" was constructed, and wars were fought in defense of "strategic interests."

For reasons of Russian history, Marxist ideology, and European tradition, Stalin's rejection of the Baruch Plan may well be seen as inevitable. But the doctrine of military superiority — stemming from the assumption of conflicting national interests — has important corollaries.

The first is that our nation's "security" is, by definition, another's "insecurity."

Another is the formula which says that a nation should only negotiate from "a position of strength." If the principle is valid for one side it obviously is valid for the other. If "strength" means military power, quantitatively measured, then negotiations on arms control could take place only at a time when both sides are equally strong and both agree that this is the case. Otherwise, one side or the other would always be in "a position of weakness."

For another thing, both sides are likely to seek a net advantage in any negotiations that do get started. The negotiating process is, by its nature, a procedure in which each side will bargain for the best deal he can get. But no major power is likely to accept the outcome of a negotiation in which there is a net advantage for the other side. The most likely outcome is stalemate.

Another corollary of the doctrine of military superiority is a powerful incentive on both sides to "keep all military options open." And there is a fundamental conflict between arms control and maximizing military options: if arms control is not about the mutual foreclosure of selected military options, it is not about anything.

Such are some of the implications for international relations of the basic assumption that strategic national interests of major powers inevitably are conflicting.

Failure of the Baruch Plan at Lake Success meant that the

United States was forced to abandon its preferred approach to the nuclear age and to adopt another: security through development of atomic energy was replaced by security through military superiority in atomic weapons. It was the old, preatomic pattern and the United States became its prisoner; traditions governing the defense of national interests could not be abandoned unilaterally any more than the armaments which symbolize the tradition could be abandoned by one side only.

So the Soviet choice of the preatomic tradition at Lake Success in the late spring of 1946 fixed events in the framework of what came to be called "cold war" for at least two decades to come.

The cold war was rearmament and alliances and ultimatums and crises and confrontations; it was trade controls and military assistance and competitive economic aid; it was espionage and subversion and propaganda; and it was a way of acting and reacting — a way of looking at things, a frame of mind, a manner of speaking, a tone of voice. In a sense the cold war was an experiment in conflict without war; all elements of national power, influence, and prestige were brought into confrontation — and all save the military element were brought into direct use.

The preatomic political and military traditions survived the advent of the nuclear age; the alternatives to an atomic arms race were not available.

7

Tragic Figure . . . Great Drama

DURING THE SPRING and summer of 1946 Oppenheimer lectured often on the Baruch Plan in an effort to build support for it. He wanted the public to understand the issues and alternatives. He wanted to stress that the United States was doing its best to face the political implications of the nuclear age. He felt the U.S. proposals should be exposed to public debate, for belief in the value of an open forum was inherent in his faith in the open society. It was implicit, too, in his commitment to rationality.

Oppenheimer traveled and spoke before professional associations and foreign policy groups, insisting that there was no tolerable alternative to an agreement merging national sovereignties in a global authority to control the uses of nuclear power. He argued rationally and persuasively; but he soon knew it was a losing gambit. In the course of the hearing Oppenheimer said:

> After the summer [1946] of work with Mr. Baruch, it became difficult even for a dedicated optimist to think that anything

would come of the negotiations in the sense of a real agreement. It was hard to believe that before it started, and the nature of the Soviet conduct — not only the kind of objections they made, but the nature of their dealings — was extremely revealing to anyone who saw it for the first time . . .[1]

As the futile proceedings at Lake Success dragged on, the "dedicated optimist" spread pessimism among his still-hopeful scientist friends. Hans Bethe, in the course of his testimony, recalled some "quite long conversations" with Oppenheimer in January 1947:

> . . . He told me then that he had given up all hope that the Russians would agree to a plan which would give security . . . Particularly he pointed out how much the Russian plan was designed to serve the Russian interests, namely to deprive us immediately of the one weapon which would stop the Russians from going into western Europe if they so chose, and not give us any guarantee on the other hand that . . . we would be safe from Russian atomic attack at some later time.[2]

Indeed, by this time Oppenheimer wanted to break off the discussions at the United Nations. After about eight months, Baruch had resigned and was succeeded by his deputy, Frederick Osborn. Oppenheimer asked urgently to see him. As Osborn told it in the hearing:

> Dr. Oppenheimer came on to tell me that there were two very serious dangers in continuing negotiations . . . he was now certain . . . that the Russians had no intention of accepting any plan for the international control of atomic energy which would mean lifting the Iron Curtain . . .
> Yet he felt certain that, if the Iron Curtain were not lifted, any plan of international control would be exceedingly dangerous to the United States. What he was afraid of was that

. . . we would accept compromises which would put the United States in a very dangerous position of not really knowing what was going on in Russia, whereas the Russians would know all about what was going on here.

This was the first danger . . . He also felt that the continuation of negotiations was something that the Russians would be glad to use . . . as a medium for propaganda, and this propaganda they could use against us . . .

So he was for discontinuing negotiations.[3]

In the early days of the great nondebate at Lake Success, Oppenheimer was struck by the impression that Gromyko had been given no authority to negotiate and those in authority in Moscow, probably were ignorant of what nuclear energy was all about. At the same time he understood well the political implications of the Baruch Plan for the Soviet system of power. In a secret lecture to the War College in September 1947, he said:

. . . I think no one can take with any seriousness the hope or expectation that the Soviet Union will accede, or will come close to acceding, to what is now the majority plan.

. . . The cornerstone of our proposal is an institution which requires candidness and great openness . . . It involves a maximum effort to abolish national rivalries in the field of atomic energy . . .

. . . The proposed pattern of control stands in a very gross conflict to the present patterns of state power in Russia . . .

What we have asked of the Russians is a very far-reaching renunciation and reversal of the basis of their state power and of their state power itself. It does not seem to me likely that we have found inducements or cajolery or threats which together are adequate to make them take this great plunge . . .

Here he touched upon the central dilemma of competi-

tive national existence in the nuclear age, which would haunt
Oppenheimer for years to come: On the one hand, international control of atomic energy stood "in very gross conflict"
with the existing political power system in the Soviet Union,
which showed no sign of change; on the other hand, atomic
technology would advance very rapidly and stockpiles of
bombs could accumulate apace. Political change and technological change seemed to be cast in radically different time
scales; it was a deeply depressing thought.

On the evening of the day, July 24, 1946, when Gromyko
flatly rejected the Baruch Plan in whole or in part, Oppenheimer and Lilienthal met in Washington and talked into
the small hours of the next morning. And when he turned
to his journal, Lilienthal noted:

> O. is in deep despair about the way things are going in the
> negotiations in New York. He sees no hope of agreement . . .
> It is difficult to record how profoundly hopeless he thinks it
> is . . .
> . . . He paced up and down in the frenetic way he has as he
> spoke in a really heart-breaking tone . . .

Lilienthal was discouraged too. As he wrote in his journal,
"to date it certainly appears that our efforts have resulted
in nothing that can save the world." But he was not quite
ready to give up hope. He said to Oppenheimer that there
are some situations in which one cannot acknowledge de-
spair.

"He took me to task for this," Lilienthal wrote, "in a gen-
tle but firm way, saying that it was this sense of a 'reservoir
of hope' that was quite wrong, for it does not exist . . ."

Indeed, the impact upon Oppenheimer of failure at Lake

Success was such that Lilienthal concluded his journal entry
on their talk that night like this:

> He is really a tragic figure; with all his great attractiveness,
> brilliance of mind. As I left him he looked so sad: "I am
> ready to go anywhere and do anything, but I am bankrupt of
> further ideas. And I find that physics, and the teaching of
> physics, which is my life, now seems irrelevant." It was this
> last that really wrung my heart. Here is the making of great
> drama; indeed, this *is* great drama.

8

The Open Mind at Bay

IT WAS THE MIDDLE of 1946 when Oppenheimer told Lilienthal that he was bankrupt of ideas as to how to control
atomic energy, but that he was still ready to go anywhere and
do anything to help cope with the nuclear age. Soon there
was a place to go and something to do.

In the autumn of 1946, Congress passed the Atomic Energy Act, President Truman appointed Lilienthal the first
chairman of the United States Atomic Energy Agency, and
Lilienthal in turn asked Oppenheimer to serve on the eight-
member General Advisory Committee provided for in the
statute. At the first meeting of the committee, Oppenheimer
was elected as chairman; and, as he would say later, "The
rule for the atom was 'Let us keep ahead . . . of the enemy.'" [1]

It was not the chosen policy of the United States Government; but it was the doctrinal straitjacket in which it was
now imprisoned. Sovereignty, security, superiority, secrecy
— these became the watchwords of the day and for many a

day thereafter. Keeping ahead was the name of the game and Oppenheimer was in the center of the play.

The new job required a new security clearance, this being the curious custom in Washington. There was no real problem about it this time: his "associations" now were with generals and admirals, college presidents, cabinet officers, investment bankers, diplomats, and other reliable types who could attest to his loyalty, security, and views about Communism. General Groves, Dr. Bush, Dr. Conant, and Secretary of War Robert Patterson all assured the atomic energy commissioners in writing that the old associations with labor organizers and left-wing intellectuals were no cause for concern about Oppenheimer. They all agreed that he should be cleared again. He was. And the bulging Oppenheimer dossier was returned by the AEC to the FBI.

The General Advisory Committee, not surprisingly, was drawn largely from the wartime scientific leadership, especially those who served on the Manhattan District Project. The committee did not, of course, have any decision-making power; it could merely offer opinions and make recommendations to the commissioners. But it was not and never was intended to be a mere panel of technicians. Only one of the AEC commissioners was a scientist by training, and since nuclear energy was a brand-new field, there was nothing to go on in the way of experience save the Hiroshima and Nagasaki bombs and the uncertain prospect of industrial power. Fermi and Oppenheimer probably knew more about atomic weapons than any other two men, and David Lilienthal, head man in the agency responsible by law for the whole atomic enterprise, leaned heavily on the advisory group and its chairman. He sought their opinions on the toughest problems before the house: whether to abandon Los Alamos and start all over again in a more normal setting; how to over-come bottlenecks in the production of fissionable materials; which alternative weapons designs looked more feasible and effective; how to lay out a program of testing — these were among the questions.

From time to time the committee offered unsolicited ad-vice to the commission on such things as general support for science in the United States and closer U.S. cooperation in nuclear affairs with Britain and Canada. Sometimes the ad-vice was followed and sometimes it wasn't, but the General Advisory Committee of the AEC, under the chairmanship of Oppenheimer, became the in-group among the nuclear scientists whom physicist Ralph Lapp would call the New Priesthood.[2] Perhaps because men who have made a revolu-tion tend to disbelieve the next revolution, members of the General Advisory Committee were destined to become con-servatives within the scientific community.

In the early years of his chairmanship, Oppenheimer could find no alternative to the simple imperative that flows from the very nature of arms competition: keep ahead of the en-emy. Yet he entered the job with certain "freight" as he put it. On the one hand was a conviction that "some day this stuff is going to put an end to major total wars." On the other was a fear that before that day arrived there might first be an exchange of nuclear weapons "on a massive scale against civilizations and cities." He was thinking, of course, in a period in which one could still conceive of "winning" a nuclear war.

From the beginning Oppenheimer fretted about two points which increasingly bothered him: the seeming irrelevance of the scientific method to the world of politics; and the impact of military secrecy upon the open society. The scientist and weapon-builder were at war within him, and evidence of conflict, though muted, can be found in his own public speeches from the earliest days of the nuclear age. The references were circumspect, low key, and usually well padded with erudite musings about the scientific heritage.

He was a master of the understatement. If he meant that something was enormously important, he was likely to say, almost as an aside, that "this is not trivial"; if he described a hope of vast ambition, he would describe it as "nothing modest."

Nevertheless, in retrospect, Oppenheimer's lectures reflect a harrowing inner struggle. The world of Göttingen and the world of the AEC seemed to be irreconcilable; the open mind was at bay.

Oppenheimer did not share the assumption, which seemed to be prevalent among some of his scientist colleagues, that the world would quickly straighten out if the politicians would only listen to the physicists. He had found, in private talks with Russian scientists in New York, that the scientific method was one thing and political ideology was something else; he knew from debate with American scientists that a shared devotion to rationality did not necessarily produce political bedfellows or even a common way of looking at national defense. Indeed, he was impatient with those of his brethren who tended to behave as though they had the answers to international harmony and world order.

In November 1947, in the course of a lecture at the Massachusetts Institute of Technology, he had some harsh words to say about this — presumably aimed at those scientists who had turned to writing and signing petitions, advertisements, and articles demanding that political leaders do something quickly about the dangers of the nuclear age. On the occasion at MIT, Oppenheimer referred to some of the things being said at the time about the relation of science to society and added:

> One of these is that the scientist should assume responsibility for the fruits of his work. I would not argue against this, but it must be clear to all of us how very modest such assumption of responsibility can be, how very ineffective it has been in the past, how necessarily ineffective it will surely be in the future. In fact, it appears little more than exhortation to the man of learning to be properly uncomfortable, and, in the worst instances, is used as a sort of screen to justify the most casual, unscholarly and, in the last analysis, corrupt intrusion of scientists into other realms of which they have neither experience nor knowledge, nor the patience to obtain them.
>
> The study of physics, and I think my colleagues in the other sciences will let me speak for them too, does not make philosopher-kings. It has not, until now, made kings. It almost never makes fit philosophers — so rarely that they must be counted as exceptions . . .
>
> . . . Surely the establishment of a secure peace is very much in all our minds. It is right that we try to bring reason to bear on an understanding of this problem; but for that there are available to us no equivalents of the experimental techniques of science. Errors of conception can remain undetected and even undefined. No means of appropriately narrowing the focus of thinking is known to us. Nor have we found good avenues for extending or deepening our experience that bears upon this problem. In short, almost all the preconditions of scientific activity are missing, and in this case, at least, one may have a melancholy certainty that man's inventiveness will not rapidly provide them . . .[3]

A few years later, on March 7, 1950, in addressing the winners of the Westinghouse Science Talent Search, Oppenheimer came back to the question: Is there anything we can learn from science that is relevant to politics? He went on:

> If we are to answer these questions and answer them honestly, we must recognize important and basic differences between problems of science and problems of action as they arise in personal or in political life. If we fail to recognize these differences, we shall be seeking magic solutions and not real ones. We shall delude ourselves into laying aside responsibility, which it is an essential part of man's life to bear.
>
> In most scientific study, questions of good and evil or right and wrong play at most a minor and secondary part. For practical decisions of policy, they are basic. Without them political action would be meaningless . . .
>
> Political decisions are unique acts. In politics there is little that can correspond to the scientist's repetition of an experiment. An experiment that fails in its purpose may be as good or better than one that succeeds, because it may well be more instructive. A political decision cannot be taken twice. All the factors that are relevant to it will conjoin only once . . .

Yet he could never quite let it go at that. The very existence of a gulf between the scientific and political processes nettled him. He could not accept the conclusion that there was nothing at all which the method and order of the scientific approach could bring to political problem-solving. He could not quite abandon Bohr's conviction that the universal outlook of scientists might somehow help the politicians steer their way around the international issues of the day.

In the same lecture at MIT in which he admonished fellow scientists against a "corrupt intrusion of scientists into other realms of which they have neither experience nor knowledge," Oppenheimer said:

> . . . Of all intellectual activity, science alone has flourished in the last centuries, science alone has turned out to have the kind of universality among men which the times require. I shall be disputed in this; but it is near to truth.
>
> . . . In physics the worker learns the possibility of error very early. He learns that there are ways to correct his mistakes; he learns the futility of trying to conceal . . .
>
> . . . It is a field in which the technique of experiment has given an almost perfect harmony to the balance between thought and action . . . We learn that views may be useful and inspiriting although they are not complete. We come to have a great caution in all assertions of totality, of finality or absoluteness.
>
> . . . We learn to throw away those instruments of action and those modes of description which are not appropriate to the reality we are trying to discern, and in this most painful discipline find ourselves modest before the world.

Again, in the speech to winners of the Westinghouse Talent Search, he said:

> . . . What we need to remember is that war today has become and is increasingly becoming, something very different from what it was a century ago or a millennium ago. We need to recognize the new situation as new; we need to come to it with something of the same spirit as the scientist's when he has conducted an experiment and finds that the results are totally other than those he had anticipated.

But the differences between political action and scientific experiment were still there, and Oppenheimer concluded his MIT lecture with these paragraphs:

We may hope for an ever-widening and more diverse field of application of science. But we must be aware how slowly these things develop and how little their development is responsive to even the most desperate of man's needs. For me it is an open question . . . whether . . . these expanding areas in which the scientific spirit can flourish may yet contribute in a decisive way to man's rational life.

I have had to leave this essential question [the relation of science to society] unanswered: I am not at all proud of that. In lieu of apology perhaps I may tell a story of another lecturer, speaking at Harvard . . . two decades ago. Bertrand Russell had given a talk on the then quantum mechanics, of whose wonders he was most appreciative. He spoke hard and earnestly in the New Lecture Hall. And when he was done, Professor Whitehead, who presided, thanked him for his efforts, and not least for leaving the vast darkness of the subject unobscured.

Oppenheimer was unaccustomed and unsuited to leaving vast darknesses unobscured. But there it was, and it was frustrating.

On the issue of military secrecy, Oppenheimer also was frustrated, but not by his own inability to see what should be done about it: he wanted to declassify all but strictly military secrets about atomic energy; he wanted to share nuclear knowledge with principal allies; and, above all, he wanted the national defense dilemmas inherent in the nuclear age to be debated publicly.

Secrecy bothered him at two levels. One was the impact of secrecy upon the progress of science. The other was the impact of secrecy upon the quality of democratic life in general. A month before the Baruch Plan was launched at the United Nations, Oppenheimer delivered a lecture before

the George Westinghouse Centennial Forum in Pittsburgh.
He referred to the "probable future technical developments
of atomic explosives" and then quickly added: ". . . But
there are things that we cannot talk about here. When, if
ever, they can be talked about openly, it will be a very different world, and to my way of thinking a very much better
one."

The main content of that lecture was an explanation of
the Acheson-Lilienthal proposals, first made public, as Secretary Byrnes had said, to "facilitate public understanding and
discussion"; but again he added that such discussion was
"made more difficult by the secrecy which has been maintained and is still maintained about many of its technical elements . . ."

As early as 1946, Oppenheimer told Lilienthal of his fear
that the pervading secrecy of a nuclear arms race with the
Soviet Union would spawn a new wave of Red-baiting and
wind up by smearing liberal thought and institutions. The
fear never left him.

In his public lectures, Oppenheimer drew upon the origins
of democratic life in Greece, upon the Age of Enlighten-
ment, upon the Founding Fathers and Jeffersonian principles — all in the context of speaking about the spirit of science. But his underlying message came through: democratic
life in the United States was endangered by the corruption
of secrecy in public affairs.

In his speech to the winners of the talent search, Oppenheimer said that "in the large, science has flourished in conditions of human freedom" and "its growth is parallel to
the growth of democratic institutions." And when he asked
rhetorically what the spirit of science could teach about
"practical affairs," he went on to say:

. . . Science is not based on authority. It owes its acceptance and its universality to an appeal to intelligible, communicable evidence that any interested man can evaluate . . .

Our own political life is predicated on openness. We do not believe any group of men adequate enough or wise enough to operate without scrutiny or without criticism. We know that the only way to avoid error is to detect it, that the only way to detect it is to be free to inquire. We know that the wages of secrecy are corruption. We know that in secrecy error, undetected, will flourish and subvert.

On public platforms, Oppenheimer wrapped his message in generalizations about the spirit of science; but behind closed doors, he went straight to the heart of it. In his lecture to the War College in 1947 he said about secrecy in nuclear science:

. . . there is the question, to which I have to return over and over again, of the proper balance between openness and security, and the necessity, if one is to look to a heroic future in this field, for cultivating and for training young men, for cultivating a corps of people who are informed and knowledgeable and useful, for establishing appropriate relations with the scientists and technical people of other countries. And there is also a manifest inadequacy in a total and uncompromising policy of security—a policy which this country has never adopted from the earliest days—to laying the foundation for any future possible internationalization . . .

In order to work well, people need to have some sense of participation in policy making; in order to make policy they have to know things; and in order to know things you have to tell them, you have to let them learn . . .

It was on that premise that Oppenheimer had violated the Manhattan District's rule of compartmentalization at Los Alamos — and got away with it. But Oppenheimer's need to tell people — to "let them learn" — would lead him into deeper and deeper trouble. On occasion he seemed to catch a foreboding glimpse of just how far it could lead. In his talk to the talent search winners he said: "To preserve the freedom of the human mind . . . every spirit should be ready to devote itself to martyrdom . . ."

9

"Security," "Strategy," and the Bomb

Oppenheimer felt free to worry out loud about the impact upon science and society of the military secrecy that came with the nuclear age. But he had much deeper worries that went to the heart of national defense policy and the military strategy that served it.

Inescapably, Oppenheimer was drawn into the military strategy business from the beginning. This was partly because the line between technical and policy advice is a faint and shifting demarcation, often indiscernible and sometimes impossible to draw. Besides, Oppenheimer was asked directly for advice on fundamental and conceptual aspects of national security policy and on supporting military strategy.

In early 1948, for example, a member of the Navy General Board, which was then launching a broad strategic study, wrote to Oppenheimer seeking his views on such sweeping questions as what kinds of wars the United States might be forced to fight in the future and how to prepare for them. In his reply Oppenheimer protested at once that this was not his forte.

"Though I am aware of the great importance which attaches to this study," he wrote, ". . . I nevertheless must protest my almost total lack of qualification for speaking to the question which you have put. Such comments as I can make should be given no great weight; they rest on little experience and little knowledge." With that out of the way, Oppenheimer proceeded to give his personal views on the military problem faced by the United States:

> Whatever our hopes for the future, we must surely be prepared, both in planning and in the development of weapons, and insofar as possible in our "forces in being," for more than one kind of conflict. That is, we must be prepared to meet the enemy in certain crucial, strategic areas in which conflict is likely, and to defeat him in those areas. We must be prepared if need be, to engage in total war, to carry the war to the enemy and attempt to destroy him. One reason why we must keep both of these objectives in mind (and they call for quite different plans and quite different emphasis as to equipment, troops and weapons) is that it may not be in our hands to decide . . .
>
>   . . . it would seem to me likely that our primary objective would be to prevent the success of Soviet arms and Soviet policies, to carry out a policy of attrition, and not to engage in a total war aimed at destroying entirely the sources of Soviet power. There are many arguments for this and I have little to add to the obvious ones. Yet, the general political consideration that the consequences, even in victory, of a total war carried out against the Soviet Union would be inimical to the preservation of our way of life, is most persuasive to me . . .[1]

This was another bit of the "freight" that Oppenheimer took with him when he joined the General Advisory Committee, and it would stay with him until the end: the United

States must be prepared for nuclear war with the Soviet Union, but if it came to conflict should seek to avoid total war; simultaneously it should be prepared with "quite different" plans, equipment, troops, and weapons for possible use in "strategic areas" of the world in which "conflict is likely."

A large number of important corollaries would flow from this proposed military posture of being prepared for "more than one kind of conflict." And so would a large number of disputes.

Even in the early days of the nuclear age, Oppenheimer's views on national security policy were not the prevailing ones. No doubt it was inescapable, once forced into competitive armament with the Soviet Union, for the United States to place heavy emphasis on atomic weapons, even if their only rational function was to guarantee their nonuse by "deterring" war. They were, after all, the "greatest military weapons in history." And the United States began with the greatest possible lead: a monopoly — even though it was assumed from the start that the monopoly would be broken. No doubt it was inescapable, too, that heavy emphasis would be placed on offensive strategic nuclear weapons: the enemy was far away and relatively invulnerable to land or sea attack.

Since nuclear science was in its infancy — and the Second World War had shown what could be done by harnessing science to the defense effort — a large part of the postwar plan to "stay ahead" would naturally be devoted to research and development of nuclear weapons technology or, more generally, to leadership on the moving frontiers of scientific discovery and invention.

The implications of all this for national defense policy were reinforced powerfully by politics, economics, and public psychology. The Strategic Air Force had emerged from the Second World War as the glamor branch of the armed services and quickly became the darling of the military and appropriations committees on Capitol Hill.

Meanwhile, the Truman administration was economizing after the heavy wartime spending by reducing the budget, cutting the deficit, and avoiding inflation in the overheated postwar economy. At the same time it was taken for granted that Congress, which wanted no part of the Universal Service Bill proposed by the administration, would not appropriate enough funds for both nuclear arms and large conventional forces.

And security through nuclear deterrence offered a relatively simple answer to the depressingly complex question of how the world's leading power should allocate its resources and design its armed forces to help keep the peace of the nuclear age.

In reality, then, Oppenheimer's proposal for a flexible military strategy did not have much more chance in the United States than his proposal for an Atomic Development Authority had in the United Nations. But if he understood why that was so, it brought him little comfort. Indeed, it frustrated and worried him.

For the fact remained — as the Chicago scientists and the Acheson-Lilienthal panel reported — that the very nature of the Great Weapons put an urbanized America at an inherent disadvantage in a nuclear-armed world, and the aggressor state held unprecedented advantages. These liabilities for the U.S. seemed so appalling to Robert Oppenheimer that he, probably alone among all the scientists, was willing to weigh the hypothetical option of what was known euphemistically as a "preemptive strike" against the Soviet Union.

As long as it was assumed that a future war could bring strategic nuclear weapons into play, there was no way around the fundamental and inherent disadvantages to the United States. To "stay ahead" was the only hope; if worst came to worst, superiority would achieve whatever might pass for victory in a nuclear exchange.

But, as Oppenheimer indicated to the Navy General Board, a nuclear war was not the only assumption available. In fact it was not the assumption of many military strategists and planners. As things turned out, the invention of atomic arms would create as much havoc in the community of professional military strategists as the discovery of the New Physics created in the community of professional physicists; donnybrooks about "strategy" would split the military services for years to come as professional military men, in the United States and elsewhere, tried to grasp what the nuclear revolution had done to their military doctrines and to the "roles and missions" of the armed services.

Feuding among soldiers, sailors, and airmen went far deeper than traditional interservice jealousies, and far beyond the familiar scramble for the largest attainable slice of the defense budget. It went directly to the basic issue of whether the United States should accept as its primary military role in any future warfare aerial bombardment of enemy targets with weapons of mass destruction, and indeed whether — apart from political and moral considerations — strategic bombing is militarily effective.

On this, the Strategic Air Command had few doubts. Its position was based on a "theory of warfare" described in the Oppenheimer hearings by Air Force Major General Roscoe Charles Wilson: "I believe," he said,

> . . . in the theories of Douhet and Mitchell and Admiral Mahan as modified to fit the present war. This is a belief that the objective of war is not the defeat of the enemy's army, but the defeat of the enemy's will to wage war . . .
>
> The USSR in the airman's view is a land power . . . I feel that it could exist for a long time without sea communications. Therefore it is not really vulnerable to attack by sea. Furthermore, it has a tremendous store of manpower . . . So my feeling is that it is relatively invulnerable to land attack.
>
> Russia is the base of international communism. This base is vulnerable only to attack by air power. I don't . . . say that only air power should be employed in case of a war with Russia but I say what strategy is established should be centered around air power.
>
> I further believe that whereas air power might be effective with ordinary weapons, the chances of success against Russia with atomic weapons or nuclear weapons are far, far greater.[2]

General Wilson did not purport to be speaking for the whole Air Force but he said that "there are a great number of people who belong to this school of thought." He was right. As far as Big Bomber generals were concerned, the basic doctrine of military superiority, as the touchstone of national security, was married to the operational doctrine of strategic bombing.

This school of thought was shared by many outside the military. Walter Millis in *Arms and the State* quotes Representative Clarence Cannon, chairman of the House Appropriations Committee to this effect:

If there should be another war . . . the outcome would be decisively determined by atomic warfare in three weeks or less. But . . . neither the Army nor the Navy could reach Moscow with the first atomic bomb in three weeks — or three years. Only land-based bombers could reach Moscow with a lethal charge . . . The only way to avoid war is to have available at any instant the means of striking swiftly . . . And the atomic bomb, serviced by land-based bombers, is the only weapon which can assure that protection.[3]

Robert Oppenheimer never accepted that much reliance on the Great Weapons as a basis for defense policy and military strategy. In the event of conventional Russian aggression in Europe the United States would have the choice of sitting by while Europe was overrun, or of starting a strategic nuclear war. To Oppenheimer both were intolerable alternatives.

Nor did it make much sense to those who took part in the so-called Admiral's Revolt of mid-1949. This affair was represented mainly as a fight between the Air Force and Navy over the relative merits of the B-36 bomber and the super aircraft carriers that the Navy wanted to build. The real issue under debate was: What strategic doctrine should guide United States defense policy?

In point of fact, Navy spokesmen laid it on the line in open hearings before the House Armed Services Committee. Admiral Arthur W. Radford, commander of the Pacific Fleet, opened his statement this way:

The kind of war we plan to fight must fit the kind of peace we want. We cannot look to the military victory alone, with no thought to the staggering problems that would be generated by the death and destruction of an atomic blitz . . . The B-36

has become, in the minds of the American people, a symbol of
a theory of warfare — the atom blitz — which promises them a
cheap and easy victory if war should come . . .

Less than 6 percent of Air Force research and development
funds is earmarked for tactical and fighter types . . . the
United States is not sound in relying on the so-called strategic
bombing concept to its present extent . . . In the minds of
our citizens this fallacious concept promises a short-cut to victory. Our citizens must realize that military leaders cannot
make this promise.[4]

Admiral R. A. Oftsie, another Navy witness before the
Armed Services Committee, said more of the same:

Much emphasis has been placed upon the instantaneous
character of an offensive using atomic bombs. Among laymen
this has produced an illusion of power and even a kind of
bomb-rattling jingoism . . . The idea that it is within our
power to inflict maximum damage to the enemy in a short time
without serious risk to ourselves created the delusion that we
are stronger than we actually are . . .[5]

In the course of the quarrel the Navy was accused of trying
to share in the strategic bombing business with large aircraft carriers. Admiral Oftsie offered much more than a jurisdictional reason for denying it: "We consider the strategic
air warfare as practiced in the past and as proposed in the
future is militarily unsound and of limited effect, morally
wrong and decidedly harmful to the stability of a post-war
world."

The admirals had their day in court. Cities, they said,
were poor targets. But that's where it stopped.

During the first few years of the atomic age, all the public
pressures — for "economy," for an easy answer to "security,"

for avoidance of a peacetime draft, for domestic price stability — pushed in the direction of heavy reliance on the nuclear deterrent. Conventional services were to split the remainder of a total defense budget with a fixed ceiling, more or less arbitrarily established in the interests of saving money.

But during the Truman administration, this was more of a practical than a doctrinal choice. National Security Council studies made appropriate noises about the roles of conventional forces; special gatherings of military chieftains met to compose disputed issues and emerged with differences partly compromised — at least on paper; strategic doctrine was still debatable within the Joint Chiefs of Staff; and even the Finletter Report of 1948 — an unabashed argument for building U.S. military strategy around the nuclear role of the Strategic Air Command — at least tipped its hat to the continuing roles of an army and a navy.

Oppenheimer, of course, was not directly involved in all of this; he was in no position to influence the allocation of budgetary resources among the competing services. But he *was* in a position to exert some influence over the kind and size and purpose of atomic weapons being designed — and this inevitably impinged upon strategy and policy.

Oppenheimer knew that atomic bombs could be made increasingly destructive with new inventions, improved technology, and better design. But he was convinced, too, that atomic weapons with smaller yields could be designed and adapted for armed services other than the Strategic Air Command — and for conflicts short of total war. In brief he was convinced that atomic weapons had a potential tactical as well as strategic role.

In the early days of the nuclear armament program, all the fissile material available was needed to start a stockpile of big bombs. But by 1948, after taking part in the first long-range study and projection of future supplies of materials, Oppenheimer foresaw a time of nuclear plenty, with enough material for a variety of nuclear weapons.

He proposed weapons of less than an order-of-magnitude jump in destructive power over conventional explosives that might be used in support of ground and naval warfare without necessarily triggering a strategic nuclear exchange in which American cities and populations would be the principal victims. The implication for strategy was that nuclear energy might be related, after all, to conventional military operations. This was about as close as Oppenheimer would come to reconciling the nuclear age with military and political traditions.

Oppenheimer's campaign for variety in the atomic weapons cupboard was described later, in the course of the Oppenheimer hearings, by Dr. Walter Whitman, head of the chemistry department of MIT and a member of the General Advisory Committee:

> . . . There had been in the early days of scarcity a very strongly held belief that the bomb was useful in strategic bombing and there had been very little thought given to the expansion of the use of the bomb for other military purposes.

> . . . I think very definitely he [Oppenheimer] felt that great emphasis should be put on having a spectrum in the arsenal of atomic weapons; that there were so many potentialities to this new material. He recognized, as practically everybody has, that the strategic use was being pushed with utmost speed.

> He felt it quite incumbent . . . to emphasize the many other

potentialities of the atomic weapon, and since that was not being talked about by others he was peculiarly conscious of his responsibility.

I should say that always Dr. Oppenheimer was trying to point out the wide variety of military uses for the bomb . . .

I should say that he, more than any other man, served to educate the military to the potentialities of the atomic weapon for other than strategic bombing purposes . . .

In my judgment his advice and his arguments for a gamut of atomic weapons, extending even to the use of atomic weapons in air defense of the United States, has been more productive than any other one individual . . .[6]

Enrico Fermi would testify to the same effect in the course of the Oppenheimer hearings:

I think I can say very definitely that I always saw him push for all the measures that could improve our position in conventional atomic weapons, and this includes seeing to it that exploration of ores would go ahead vigorously, that production of primary materials would be expanded, that all the various gadgets that go into this weapon would be streamlined as much as possible, that varieties of weapons that could conceivably improve our military position would be investigated and developed . . .[7]

Fermi added that promotion of new kinds of nuclear weapons tended to fall to the two members of the GAC who knew most about the technical details of weapons — "Oppenheimer first and I, in a somewhat second line."

Thus Oppenheimer, the father of the first bomb to wipe out a city, became, in turn, the sponsor of a "family" of atomic weapons designed for lesser missions.

This role did not win him friends among the Big Bomber

generals, or among the civilian heads of the Air Force, or among the scientists committed to ever-increasing yields from improved strategic weapons. As Dr. Whitman said in the course of the same testimony:

> . . . In the early days there was such a strong feeling that the bomb was the peculiar and sole property of the Strategic Air Command. It was very necessary to open up the minds of the military to other potential uses of this material . . . The Strategic Air Command had thought of the atomic weapon as solely restricted to its own use. I think that there was some definite resentment at the implication that this was not just the Strategic Air Command's weapon.[8]

There were other sources of resentment, as General Wilson would testify during the Oppenheimer hearings. The Air Force was not grateful for some of the technical advice it was getting and General Wilson gave some examples. One had to do with the development of a range of "devices" for detecting atomic detonations in the Soviet Union. "The Air Force felt," General Wilson said, "that it required quite an elaborate system of devices . . . Dr. Oppenheimer was not enthusiastic about two or three of these devices or systems . . ."

Another example of unwelcome opinion, cited by General Wilson was this:

> Dr. Oppenheimer also opposed the nuclear powered aircraft . . . but at the same time he felt less strongly opposed to the nuclear powered ships. The Air Force feeling was that at least the same energy should be devoted to both projects.[9]

Not that any great damage was done: the "devices" selected for detecting distant atomic detonations turned out to work very well; the GAC supported work on nuclear reactors for submarines; and the Air Force plowed ahead in its efforts to develop a nuclear-powered bomber until, about a billion dollars later, the project was canceled by President Kennedy.

In any event, resentment against Oppenheimer in high echelons of SAC began early and accumulated. Some of it was too frivolous to be explained — except in the light of larger issues of military policy.

10

Too Big for the Target

Toward the end of summer 1949, the crew of a special Air Force plane, on patrol over the Bering Sea, found the evidence it and other such crews had been looking for: apparent traces of radioactive materials in clouds drifting from west to east. The suspicious cloud bank was followed as it moved across the northern United States and Canada. En route air samples were scooped systematically and then rushed to Washington for urgent analysis.

Lilienthal records in his journals how he was tracked down just before midnight of the following day in a remote vacation cottage on Cape Cod. His unexpected visitor was the chief of the AEC's intelligence unit; and over a bottle of beer in the cottage kitchen, Lilienthal heard of the evidence that the Soviet Union might have detonated its first nuclear device. At dawn he started back to Washington in a special aircraft sent to a nearby airport to fetch him.

When Lilienthal arrived at his office, there was still some doubt among the experts about the evidence; not everyone was convinced. But Oppenheimer, who had been called at once to help analyze the samples, had no doubt whatever: the Russians had "the secret" of Los Alamos; the American atomic monopoly was a piece of history; Stalin had his hands on the Great Weapon; the "strategic balance" would be al-tered radically; and the doctrine of deterrence would have to prove itself in a brand-new environment.

According to Lilienthal's journal, Oppenheimer appeared "frantic, drawn." [1] And when Oppenheimer shortly was called to verify the evidence before the Joint Committee on Atomic Energy, Senator Vandenberg posed the central ques-tion for an agonized debate that would go on for nearly four months in the secret councils of Washington: "Doctor, what do we do now?"

There were some who had no doubts at all as to what should be done now. For example, Dr. Wendell Latimer, professor of chemistry at the University of California and associate director of the Radiation Laboratory at Berkeley, described in the course of the Oppenheimer hearings his own reactions to the news of Soviet accession to atomic power:

> I felt that it was only a question of time that the Russians got the A-bomb . . . It also seemed to me obvious that the logical thing for them to do was to shoot immediately for the super weapon [H-bomb]. So . . . I started worrying about the fact that we seemed to be twiddling our thumbs and doing nothing.[2]

Dr. Latimer said that "it was not directly my business" to know what was going on in the nuclear weapons field and "it was not my job to be working on it," but "I saw Teller occasionally" and from "a lot of sources of classified infor-

mation" he gained "impressions" and derived "suspicions."
And, as he put it:

> As time passed I got more and more anxious. I talked to
> a good many people about it . . .
> I talked to Glenn Seaborg for one. I didn't get much satis-
> faction out of the answers. They seemed to me most of them on
> the phony side . . .
> I felt so certain that the Russians would get the A-bomb and
> shoot for the H-bomb that all during that period I probably
> was over-anxious, at least compared to most of the scien-
> tists . . .
> . . . When the Russians exploded their first A-bomb, then
> I really got concerned . . . I got hold of Ernest Lawrence
> and I said, "Listen, we have to do something about it." . . .
> the same afternoon Dr. Alvarez got hold of him and told him
> the same thing. I guess the two of us working on him at once
> with different impulses got him excited, and the three of us
> went to Washington that week-end to attend another meeting
> and we started talking the best we could, trying to present our
> point of view to various men in Washington . . .

"Around the [Atomic Energy] Commission . . . I talked
largely to the chemistry group . . ." Dr. Latimer said he
had a "good many friends . . . such as Ken Pitzer" and added
that Dr. Pitzer "didn't take very long" to agree with him
about the H-bomb. Meanwhile, Dr. Latimer said, "Dr. Lawrence and Dr. Alvarez talked to a good many other men . . .
members of the Joint Congressional Committee and various
men in the Air Force and Army.

> . . . I tried to build up pressure for it. I definitely tried to
> build up pressure for it . . .
> Granted at that time the odds of making a super weapon
> were not known . . . when the very existence of the Nation

was involved, I didn't care what the odds were . . . The stakes
were too big. The very existence of the country was involved
and you can't take odds on such things."

Lawrence and Alvarez went together to see Senator Mc-
Mahon, chairman of the Joint Congressional Committee on
Atomic Energy, to convey their concern that the Soviets
might be placing top priority on the development of a thermonuclear bomb that could put the Russians ahead in the
nuclear arms race. They pointed out that the Soviet scientist Pytor Kapitza, a former collaborator of Rutherford's at
the Cavendish Laboratory, was one of the world's leading
authorities on the physical properties of light elements and
that with his help the Soviets might perfect a hydrogen bomb
before the United States could do so.

Lawrence and Alvarez also went to work on some of the
nuclear scientists. Dr. Rabi told, in the Oppenheimer hearing, how they had come to see him in New York, after the
Russian explosion, to discuss the Super: ". . . They were
extremely optimistic about it. They had been to Los Alamos and talked to Dr. Teller, who gave them a very optimistic estimate about the thing . . . So they were all keyed up
to go bang into it." [3]

Dr. Teller subsequently called on Senator McMahon to
lobby on behalf of a crash program, along the lines of the
Manhattan Project, to create and build a thermonuclear
weapon. And somewhat later a deputation from the joint
committee went to Los Alamos and Berkeley to discuss the
H-bomb question. At that time Lilienthal noted in his journal:

Reports from Los A. and Berkeley are rather awful: the
visiting firemen saw a group of scientists who can only be

described as drooling with the prospect and "bloodthirsty."
E. O. [Lawrence] quite bad: there's nothing to think over; this
calls for the "spirit of Groves," and the ground is laid for the
Joint Committee members to come back and demand that we
plunge ahead . . .[4]

Not that the atomic energy commissioners and others were
not considering the problem. The difficulty was that the answer did not seem so self-evident to everyone as it had to
Dr. Latimer and some of the others; indeed the issue was so
tortured that Chairman Lilienthal urged his commissioners
to try to think the thing through and come to individual conclusions on their own — a departure from his normal practice of seeking a consensus among them.

Lilienthal, a professional public administrator, had felt
from the beginning that the five-man commission structure
designed by Congress for running the atomic energy program was an "administrative cretin," hardly designed to
cope with as complex a policy problem as the Super issue.
But Lilienthal was practiced in the art of engineering consensus; he had labored hard in the early years of the AEC
to make it work. By persuasion, compromise, and informal
techniques he tried to shepherd the commissioners toward
unanimous agreement on the issues before them and away
from confrontations requiring a formal commission vote.
On the whole he had been quite successful.

What friction there was came from one of the commissioners — Admiral Lewis L. Strauss, a disciplined, religious,
and self-righteous man, never in doubt as to the integrity
and correctness of his views. He was an investment banker
who had acquired the rank of rear admiral during wartime
service in the procurement division of the Navy. He had

helped and protected some of the refugee scientists and had acquired an early interest in the prospects for atomic energy. When President Truman asked him to serve on the first AEC, Strauss says in his memoirs he told the President that he was a "black Hoover Republican." The appointment was offered and accepted nonetheless.

Commissioner Strauss subsequently became a minority of one on a number of problems before the AEC during the early years. When he disagreed with the other four commissioners, he argued for appealing the case to the Secretary of State or even to the President. At times he took his own point of view to those in the Pentagon whom he knew would agree with him and to members of the joint committee — a practice known in Washington as "the end run." Strauss also seemed to feel a special duty to keep the Republican members of the joint committee fully apprised of everything that happened within the commission. But personal relations within the commission were kept on an even keel; and it was Admiral Strauss who, in early 1947, recruited Oppenheimer to become director of the Institute for Advanced Study at Princeton, New Jersey.

In any event, Strauss was the first member of the AEC to reach a firm conclusion about how to react to the Soviet A-bomb. On October 5, less than two weeks after the President had confirmed the Soviet success, Strauss addressed the following memorandum to his colleagues of the commission:

> The purpose of this memorandum is to raise a question for immediate consideration in the light of the information as to progress which has been apparently made in Russia.
> In the days since the President's announcement, I have found a tendency in my own thinking to resort to the prospect of

increased production of fissionable material and weapons as the logical procedure. Although this is very important, I feel strongly that it is not enough. The frequently expressed thought that we must "maintain our lead" is generally taken to mean that we must have a larger stockpile of weapons than the Russians because we began sooner and make them faster. Of those considerations, however, only the fact that we began sooner can be relied upon absolutely. And, in any case, we can only maintain our lead in some arithmetical difference since our relative lead is most likely to decrease.

It seems to me that the time has now come for a quantum jump in our planning (to borrow a metaphor from our scientist friends) — that is to say, we should now make an intensive effort to get ahead with the super. By intensive effort, I am thinking of a commitment in talent and money comparable, if necessary, to that which produced the first atomic weapon. That is the way to stay ahead.[5]

Oppenheimer did not find a quantum jump as easy or desirable. When the Russians detonated their first atomic device in September 1949, the Super was still a hypothetical weapon in the minds of scientists at the Los Alamos laboratory; many were skeptical as to whether the theoretical model on which they were working would ever prove out. At least some physicists believed that irreconcilable laws of nature would prevent man-made fusion; some feared that a thermonuclear explosion would get out of control and consume the planet in self-sustaining firestorms; some, like Dr. Bethe, merely hoped it would prove impossible. Even if it were possible, Oppenheimer was not sure, as he noted in a letter to Dr. Conant, whether an H-bomb could be delivered to a target in "anything except an ox cart."

Alvarez would complain later in the course of the hearings that this was not the kind of attitude which had produced the "spirit of Los Alamos" during the war. Dr. Teller also testified about a sense of impatience among some of the scientists because, he said:

> First of all, people were interested in going on with the thermonuclear device because during the war it had been generally understood that this was one of the things that the laboratory was to find out some time. It was a sort of promise in all our minds.
>
> Another thing was that the people there [Los Alamos] were a little bit tired . . . of going ahead with minor improvements and wanted to, in sort of an adventuresome spirit, go into a new field . . .[6]

Among those with the adventuresome spirit were Alvarez and Lawrence. In testifying about his visit with them and their discussion about the prospects for a super weapon, Rabi had this to say: ". . . I generally find myself when I talk with these two gentlemen in a very uncomfortable position. I like to be an enthusiast. I love it. But those fellows are so enthusiastic that I have to be a conservative . . ."[7]

Meanwhile the "minor improvements" in atomic weaponry that proved fretful to Teller and some of his associates already had produced bombs with yields of six to seven times the force of the Hiroshima weapon. Rapid advances had been made in the efficiency and economy of producing fissionable materials. More importantly, some thought, the flexible family of weapons designed for multiple missions appeared highly promising. In short, the prospects in the nuclear arsenal seemed excellent to members of the General Advisory Committee of the AEC. Besides, qualified nuclear physicists available to work on the nuclear weapons program were in short supply. As Fermi said later in the course of the Oppenheimer hearings, ". . . I was concerned that it [the Super project] might weaken the development of conventional atomic weapons which was then picking up and essentially set it back . . ." [8]

Dr. Hartley Rowe, engineer and vice president of the United Fruit Company, another member of the General Advisory Committee in 1949, covered the same point in his testimony: "I was rather loath to enter into a crash program on the H-bomb until we had more nearly perfected the military potentialities of the A-bomb . . ." [9]

Dr. Lee DuBridge, president of the California Institute of Technology and GAC member, also recalled his thoughts: ". . . it was my impression that the super design, which was then being considered was . . . in too early a stage to embark on a large and expensive program. In other words, there were technical reasons why a crash program at that time seemed unwise . . ." [10]

Dr. Oliver E. Buckley, a physicist and former chairman of the board of Bell Telephone Laboratories, also was a member of the General Advisory Committee at the time. In the course of the Oppenheimer hearings he, too, recalled that he had opposed an all-out pursuit of the Super bomb partly because of "our ignorance of how to build the Super or whether it could in fact be built at all" and because of "the great cost in money which it represented and the diversion of effort from the A-bomb program which it must mean . . ." [11]

Yet, feasibility was not the most painful issue to be faced in connection with the H-bomb. In fact the General Advisory Committee later reached a consensus to the effect that if enough resources were invested in a crash program the chances were something better than fifty-fifty that a thermonuclear bomb could be developed within five years. As it turned out, the model on which the scientists at Los Alamos were working at that time never did prove feasible, but a hydrogen bomb was in fact developed, with the benefit of new ideas, in less than five years.

More fundamental questions were being asked in 1949, questions that challenged the very purpose of an H-bomb even if it could be built quickly and easily.

The first operational atomic bomb had wiped out a city with a blast equivalent of 20,000 tons of TNT; its yield, then, was 20 kilotons. By the time the Soviets set off their first atomic device, apparently of roughly the same force, the U.S. had developed atomic bombs with yields up to 150 kilotons and still larger weapons were in prospect. But the yield of a hydrogen bomb, if one could be built, would be measured in equivalents of a million tons of TNT; its yield, then, would be stated in megatons.

That brought up a practical question, illuminated briefly but starkly by the following passage from the transcript of the Oppenheimer hearings:

AEC COUNSEL: Would you have supported the dropping of a thermonuclear bomb on Hiroshima?
OPPENHEIMER: It would make no sense at all.
AEC COUNSEL: Why?
OPPENHEIMER: The target is too small.[12]

This exposed a fundamental problem Oppenheimer had with the Super: it was too big for use against military targets — too big for any target save a few great metropolitan centers — too big for any purpose save the obliteration of urban life.

A fusion bomb with a yield of a thousand Hiroshimas would indeed provide the quantum jump that Strauss was recommending. This, of course, was what Teller had in mind when he testified in Congress about the prospect of a weapon which would be to the A-bomb what the A-bomb was to TNT. A fusion bomb would represent a thermonuclear revolution on top of the nuclear revolution of only four years before; an atomic age would give way to a thermonuclear age.

And this was not the end of it. There is no theoretical limit to the amount of destructive force that could be packed into a weapon exploded by the fusion of light-weight atoms; if the engineering problems could be solved, yields could be raised indefinitely. It was enough to make a man wonder.

Dr. Rabi, who was serving on the General Advisory Committee at the time, testified at the Oppenheimer hearing about some of the questions that bothered him about the Super:

> . . . there was the question of the military value of this weapon. One of the things which we talked about a great deal was . . . what sort of military weapon was it anyway? What sort of target it was good for . . .
>
> In other words we felt that this was not just a weapon . . . we discussed a great deal what were you buying if you got this thing . . .[13]

Hartley Rowe had similar doubts. On the same occasion, speaking of the Super, he said:

> I don't think it has any place in a military campaign at all . . . if you used it in retaliation, you are using it against civilization, and not against the military.

. . . I don't like to see women and children killed wholesale because the male element of the human race are so stupid that they can't get out of war and keep out of war." [14]

Dr. Buckley had similar thoughts:

. . . It was, I thought, a possible retaliatory weapon, one of doubtful value. It represented the diversion of effort from the area of practical military weapons to the end only of extensive genocide and ruthless destruction . . .[15]

Dr. Bush had another point:

. . . I think it is fully evident that the hydrogen bomb was of great value to Russia — much greater value to Russia than to us. I think I can also be sure that a test by us of a hydrogen bomb would be of advantage to Russia in the prosecution of their nuclear program . . .

. . . we have very little need for a 10 megaton hydrogen bomb. The Russians, on the other hand, have the great targets of New York and Chicago . . . It is of enormous advantage to them.[16]

As Oppenheimer had said of his early days at Göttingen, the aftermath of the first Soviet atomic device was "a time of great soul-searching" for some of the physicists. Shortly after learning the news, Teller went to Bethe at Ithaca to urge him to return to Los Alamos and work on the fusion project. As Bethe told of it in the course of the Oppenheimer hearings:

At the time Dr. Teller visited me, I had very great internal conflicts [about] what I should do . . .

. . . it seemed to me that it was a very terrible undertaking to develop a still bigger bomb, and I was entirely undecided and had long discussions with my wife.

... I was deeply troubled ... It seemed to me that the development of thermonuclear weapons would not solve any of the difficulties that we found ourselves in, and yet I was not quite sure whether I should refuse.

Bethe took Teller with him and went to see Oppenheimer at Princeton, looking for advice. As he recalled it: ". . . I found Dr. Oppenheimer equally undecided and equally troubled in his mind about what should be done. I did not get from him the advice I was hoping to get . . ." [17]

Oppenheimer indeed remained "troubled in his mind" after his first "grim" reaction to the Russian bomb. He was highly skeptical about the theoretical basis on which Teller and others were proceeding at Los Alamos. He was fearful that a major new weapons program would divert resources from work under way, compete for talent in short supply, disrupt the work of the existing weapons laboratory and depress the morale of Los Alamos scientists.

But he had more fundamental reasons to be troubled: thermonuclear weapons would only compound the special military advantage of an aggressor in the atomic age, and hasten the day when irreparable damage could be done by both sides without bringing any closer the day for political change in the Communist world. An H-bomb, too big for a target of 200,000 people, had no conceivable mission save in total war.

Meanwhile, thermonuclear weapons would do nothing to dispel the prenuclear political and military traditions which could not be reconciled with the destructive potential of the atomic age.

From all points of view, the prospective birth of a thermonuclear age struck Oppenheimer as a dismally retrograde event. If U.S. physicists could master the fusion process, so could the Russians sooner or later; if the U.S. built H-bombs, so would the Russians; and if the U.S. tested a successful thermonuclear device first, the Russians could learn enough from it to shortcut their own development program.

Immediately after the Soviet atomic test, Oppenheimer began canvassing the pros and cons in personal discussions at Princeton with Bethe, Teller, and with available members of the GAC. He wrote to solicit the views of another member of the committee, Glenn Seaborg, in California. He also wrote to "Uncle Jim" Conant, who was not a member but whose advice, Oppenheimer wrote, would make him feel more comfortable.

George Kennan, then director of the Policy Planning Staff of the Department of State, went to Princeton to discuss the problems of the Super with Oppenheimer in the fall of 1949. Kennan testified that in his meeting with Oppenheimer "the entire effort" was "to try to identify the considerations that were relevant to the problem to see what we had that we could really hang onto in approaching the decision." He said that "I talked more about my own views" than Oppenheimer did about his. But from what Oppenheimer did say, Kennan gained "the impression of a man who was greatly troubled by what he felt to be the extremely solemn implications of this decision . . . Who realized that it was one, the implications of which might carry very far. That it was almost impossible to predict where we might end up if this sort of a race with weapons of mass destruction were to go on indefinitely, and therefore was greatly troubled and concerned . . ." [18]

Perhaps the most intensive dialogue in Oppenheimer's

private soundings on the Super issue took place with John von Neumann, with whom he debated the subject on several occasions at Princeton. Von Neumann was developing, for the Institute for Advanced Study, a very fast computer to work on otherwise insoluble calculating problems connected with thermonuclear theory; he was an advocate of a crash program for developing the Super. In the course of the hearings, Von Neumann recalled Oppenheimer's anxieties at the time.

One was that the United States was then in a position to "saturate" the Soviet Union with atomic weapons, while the Soviet Union was far from being able to saturate U.S. targets since they had just detonated their first atomic device. "Therefore," as Von Neumann described Oppenheimer's views, "a large increment on both sides would merely mean that both sides could saturate the other," and ". . . since there was now this possibility for a large increment in destructive power, this was now for the second time, and possibly for the last time, an opportunity to try to negotiate control and disarmament." [19]

Before crossing the threshold from the atomic age to the thermonuclear age, Oppenheimer reverted to Niels Bohr's hope prior to the advent of the atomic age: it should be easier to negotiate an agreement not to build a weapon before it existed than to give them up after one or both sides had them installed in their arsenals.

Bethe agreed that the possibility of a thermonuclear age should be seized as an opportunity for another crack at the control problem. As he said in the course of the hearings:

> I thought that the alternative might be, or should be, to try once more for an agreement with the Russians, to try once

more to shake them out of their indifference or hostility . . .
and to try once more to get an agreement that that time neither
country would develop this weapon . . .[20]

Fermi testified to much the same effect in the course of the
Oppenheimer hearings.

Rabi also said that he had agreed with the view that "the
whole discussion raised an opportunity for the President of
the United States to make some political gesture . . . [to]
strengthen our moral position, should we decide to go ahead
with it. That our position should be such that depending
on the reaction, we would go ahead or not." [21]

DuBridge testified in similar vein; and Rowe put the point
in somewhat more general terms:

> My position was always against the development of the
> H-bomb.
> . . . I may be an idealist but I don't see why any people can
> go from one engine of destruction to another, each of them a
> thousand times greater in potential destruction, and still retain
> any normal perspective in regard to their relationships with
> other countries and also in relationship with peace . . .[22]

Apparently at Oppenheimer's suggestion, Secretary Acheson ordered a thorough review of the negotiating history on
international control at the United Nations to try to determine whether any purpose might be served by reopening
talks with the Russians — whether any acceptable shift in
U.S. positions or foreseeable shifts in Soviet positions might
bring the two sides within the range of a possible accommodation. The inquiry was not productive.

The General Advisory Committee of the Atomic Energy
Commission was called into session in late October of 1949

to canvass the state of atomic art in the United States in the light of atomic weapons in Russia. The AEC, in effect, put to the advisory committee the broad question: Are we doing everything that we could be doing in the nuclear weapons field? And it put a second question as a specific corollary of the first: If not, should one of the additional things be an all-out program to develop a thermonuclear weapon?

The committee met in Washington for three days, beginning October 29, with all members present except Glenn Seaborg, who had a commitment in Sweden. As usually happened, the sessions began with the chairman of the AEC present to explain how the commission wanted its advisers to focus on the subject before the house. And as sometimes happened, the committee also called in high officials of the State and Defense Departments to get their views. In this case, General Omar Bradley, then chairman of the Joint Chiefs of Staff, met with the committee; and according to Lilienthal's journal, Bradley said that there was no military requirement for a Super bomb, but he thought it might be a useful "psychological weapon." General Bradley also informed the committee members that the military chiefs believed the most dangerous point in U.S.-Soviet relations would come in about three to four years' time, presumably on the assumption that the Soviets by then would have a significant nuclear arsenal.

In due course, the General Advisory Committee settled down to its own deliberations. Oppenheimer began with Fermi at one side and went around the table calling on each member to offer his ideas in turn.

Dr. DuBridge recalled the occasion in some detail in the course of the Oppenheimer hearings:

. . . Dr. Oppenheimer did not express his point of view on this question until after all the rest of the members of the Committee had expressed themselves. It was clear, however . . . as we went around the table, that while there were differing points of view, different reasons, different methods of thinking, different methods of approach to the problem, each member came essentially to the same conclusion, namely there were better things the United States could do at that time than to embark upon this super program . . .

After they were all on the table, the Chairman said he also shared the views of the Committee . . .[23]

In the end, the committee agreed unanimously that the answer to the general question — are we doing all that we can and should do? — was no. It also agreed unanimously on a number of specific recommendations for improvement, expansion, and diversification of atomic weapons production and for increased output of fissionable materials, including the construction of new types of plants.

As for a crash program for a Super bomb, the GAC produced a very short agreed statement of one and a half pages, mainly devoted to a description of the project as it then stood and the steps that would have to be taken to design, build, and test a model. The report stated that a hydrogen weapon would be uneconomical except for use against the largest targets and that even for such targets it might not be economical in terms of damage per dollar. The key sentences in the concluding part read:

We all hope that by one means or another, the development of these weapons can be avoided. We are all reluctant to see the United States take the initiative in precipitating this development. We are all agreed that it would be wrong at the present moment to commit ourselves to an all-out effort towards its development.[24]

Two supplementary statements were appended to the report. One was signed by Conant, DuBridge, Buckley, and Oppenheimer, and its final paragraph said:

In determining not to proceed to develop the super bomb, we see a unique opportunity of providing by example some limitations on the totality of war and thus of eliminating the fear and arousing the hope of mankind.[25]

The second annex was signed by Fermi and Rabi; it said:

The fact that no limits exist to the destructiveness of this weapon makes its very existence and the knowledge of its construction a danger to humanity as a whole. It is necessarily an evil thing considered in any light. For these reasons, we believe it important for the President of the United States to tell the American public and the world that we think it is wrong on fundamental ethical principles to initiate the development of such a weapon.[26]

According to a notation in Lilienthal's journal, Dr. Conant's reaction to the Super debate was, "This whole discussion makes me feel I was seeing the same film, and a punk one, for the second time." [27]

The committee had merely supplied recommendations; decisions were for higher authority. But if it was inevitable that the director of the laboratory which produced the A-bomb would come to symbolize that achievement, it may have been inevitable, too, that the chairman of the General Advisory Committee, which recommended against a crash program for the Super, would come to symbolize opposition to the H-bomb. Inevitable or not, from the autumn of 1949 onward, J. Robert Oppenheimer became — in the minds of many in the Pentagon, in the weapons laboratories, and on Capitol Hill — the leader of a struggle against the H-bomb.

11

A Depressing World

AEC CHAIRMAN Lilienthal was opposed to the Super project
from the very beginning to the bitter end. Late in October
he noted in his journal:

> At present the issue seems to me fairly simple, and fairly
> conclusive: this would *not* further the common defense, and it
> might harm us, by making the prospects of the other course —
> toward peace — even less good than they now are. The dif-
> ference between what we have or are working on [A-bombs]
> and this [an H-bomb] is one of kind. There is no scientific, or
> non-military by-product — it is straight gadget-making.[1]

A few days later Lilienthal and the other AEC commissioners had a long discussion with Senator McMahon about
the Super, and he wrote this note about it:

> Last evening the five of us spent a couple of hours, in my
> office, with Senator McMahon. Pretty discouraging. What he
> is talking is the inevitability of war with the Russians, and what
> he says adds up to one thing: blow them off the face of the

earth, quick, before they do the same to us — and we haven't much time.

. . . The whole world revolves around the exploding atom, as he sees it — that's the whole of it, and there is no hope.[2]

In another note in his journals:

. . . discussion in the emotional atmosphere following the President's announcement of the Russian bomb on September 23rd confirms my feeling that we are all giving far too high a value to atomic weapons, little, big, or biggest; that just as the A-bomb obscured our view and gave a false sense of security, we are in danger of falling into the same error again . . . [looking for] some cheap easy way out.[3]

Lilienthal called Oppenheimer and a few other members of the General Advisory Committee who were available on short notice to return to Washington for a full exploration with the AEC commissioners of the conclusions reached by the GAC. Oppenheimer also went up to Capitol Hill to appear before the joint committee in executive session and explain the reasoning behind the committee's recommendations.

The AEC commissioners were originally split four to one on the Super issue, with Admiral Strauss as the only advocate of a "quantum jump." As debate and discussion continued, Commissioner Gordon Dean, a close friend of Senator McMahon's, came over to the Strauss side of the argument; when opinions were forwarded to the White House on November 9, two commissioners were in favor of a crash development project and three were against it.

Lilienthal felt that the issues raised went beyond the competence and responsibilities of the AEC. He called upon Secretary Acheson to argue that the decision could only be made by the President in consultation with the Secretary of State and the Secretary of Defense.

Lilienthal spoke of pressures to go thermonuclear. The joint committee on Capitol Hill was "steamed up on the subject," he said. Acheson asked if he meant that "we may be forced to follow this course whether we want to or not." Lilienthal replied that that was just the point and later noted in his journal the reaction of the Secretary of State: "What a depressing world it is," said Acheson, "looking quite gray." [4]

President Truman subsequently appointed a special three-man committee of the National Security Council to advise him: Secretary of State Acheson, Secretary of Defense Louis Johnson, and AEC Chairman Lilienthal. Under Acheson's chairmanship, the committee began a series of meetings while their staffs ground out supporting studies.

Secretary Johnson had no doubts from the very beginning: the thing to do was to waste no time in getting on with the Super. By now it had the support of the Joint Chiefs of Staff.

Secretary Acheson reserved his view. He was unsatisfied with a long study produced by the Joint Chiefs which, according to Lilienthal's journals, was "beautifully rendered" but "didn't clear things up at all." [5] Acheson put some hard questions to the Joint Chiefs about the military utility of a hydrogen bomb, and he seemed to lean toward a broad strategic reappraisal before deciding whether to enter on a radical upward spiral of the nuclear arms race.

Lilienthal advocated this view, but before the secret deliberations of the committee could run their course, word got out in public that the U.S. was facing a decision as to whether to start work on some kind of super weapon.

The leak was one of the more bizarre episodes in a long charade about atomic secrecy. Senator "Big Ed" Johnson of Colorado, in an appearance on a Sunday afternoon television panel, was arguing in favor of tighter security measures to protect atomic secrets. Suddenly he announced that the U.S. already had bombs six or seven times as powerful as the Hiroshima bomb and that the scientists at Los Alamos were working on one a thousand times more powerful — which could only mean the H-bomb. Both facts — and they were, of course, facts — were top secret matters at the time.

The information was out, and President Truman soon confirmed at a press conference that the administration was indeed confronted with a decision about a new type of atomic weapon. Pressures increased; Dr. Harold Urey made a speech predicting that the Soviet Union would build Super bombs, then deliver an irresistible ultimatum to the Western world and open the era of universal Communism. Congressmen, including Senators Connally and Bridges, came out for a quick and favorable decision to go for the Super and so did Bernard Baruch. The Joint Congressional Committee on Atomic Energy announced it would start hearings on the subject of a hydrogen bomb.

Meanwhile, as the three-man committee of the National Security Council went about its assignment from the President, the Super was being promoted within the government. Commissioner Strauss talked again with Senator McMahon and found that the senator had written to President Truman concluding, as Admiral Strauss recalled it in his memoirs, that "if the Russians should produce the thermonuclear weapon first, the results would be catastrophic, whereas if we should produce it first, there was at least a chance for protecting ourselves." The senator also argued in his letter to the President that "there was no moral distinction between the use of a single weapon causing great loss of life and heavy damage and the use of a series of smaller weapons with the same aggregate result and destruction" — pointing to the raids on Hamburg and Tokyo as being "no less lethal than the raids on Hiroshima and Nagasaki." [6]

On November 25, Strauss personally wrote the President, saying that he felt it "proper" for him to state his own views "on my own responsibility and in my own words." He attached his "premises" and "conclusions" which included the view that ". . . until disarmament is universal, our arsenal must be not less well equipped than with the most potent weapons that our technology can devise." He was not disconcerted by the vision of a weapon too big for military targets: indeed one of the conclusions he listed in his letter to the President was a claim for the Super which probably is unique in all the literature on the subject: ". . . The weapon may be critically useful against a large enemy force both as a weapon of offense and as a defensive measure to prevent landings on our own shores." [7]

Dr. Karl T. Compton, then chairman of the Research and Development Board of the Department of Defense, also wrote to the President on the same day that the views of the AEC commissioners were forwarded to the White House. Referring to the advice of the General Advisory Committee, Compton said, in part:

In the absence of a strong international agreement, backed by adequate inspection, it is clear that Russia could proceed with the development of this [super atom bomb] type of weapon

quite irrespective of any high-minded decisions and announce-
ments on our part. There is no basic scientific secret standing
in the way and there are some brilliant atomic scientists among
the Russians and collaborating Germans.

While I should hope that we can keep well ahead of the
Russians, I think we are more likely to underestimate than to
overestimate their capacity. Certainly we will not keep ahead
of them in this particular project if we renounce it and they
work on it.

Therefore, until an adequate international solution is worked
out, it seems to me that our own national security and the
protection of the type of civilization which we value, requires
us to proceed with the development of the most powerful
atomic weapons which may be in sight . . .[8]

By the time the Special Committee of the National Security Council met for a decisive session on January 30, 1950,
Secretary Acheson had reached the view that public pressures would not permit the delay required for the high-level
review of security policy favored by himself and Lilienthal.
He believed that a deliberate and comprehensive policy review could hardly take place in an atmosphere of public tension; that a decision to explore on a priority basis the feasibility of a thermonuclear weapon could be taken without
necessary prejudice to a later decision whether to build
such a weapon; and that security policy could be reviewed
in the interim.

In that final meeting of the special committee, Lilienthal
restated his position and argued that a prior decision to start
down the road toward thermonuclear weapons could not fail
to prejudice the outcome of a security study in favor of continued reliance on the most powerful weapons of mass destruction. But he volunteered the opinion that his own views

would carry no weight against those of the Secretaries of State and Defense. So the three men drafted a proposed presidential statement and, with this in hand, headed for the White House for an appointment with the President. Secretary Acheson handed Mr. Truman the joint recommendations of the two cabinet officers and said that Chairman Lilienthal had some remarks to make.

President Truman, who of course knew where Lilienthal stood, plainly had made his decision. He turned at once to Lilienthal and said that while "our whole purpose was peace," and that while "we should never use these weapons," nonetheless "we had to go on and make them because of the way the Russians were behaving; we had no other choice." [9]

Lilienthal then went through the motions of stating the case for the opposition and the meeting was over. Before the day was out the White House announced that the President had directed the Atomic Energy Commission "to continue its work on all forms of atomic weapons, including the so-called hydrogen or super-bomb . . ."

Lilienthal returned to the AEC offices to break the news to the members of the General Advisory Committee, who were assembled waiting for the word — which by now was foreshadowed. "It was like a funeral," he wrote in his journal that night.

Lilienthal told the others that he would not challenge the President's decision in public and neither should they. Then Oppenheimer, seconded by others, suggested that perhaps it would be better if the advisory committee were to resign in view of its unanimous recommendation against priority for the Super. Lilienthal pleaded with them not to do so; and he later relayed to Oppenheimer a request from the Secretary of State not to "upset the applecart" by tendering a resignation.

After making his notes on the day's events, Lilienthal concluded that entry in his journal on a subjective note:

> No denying, this is a night of heartache. But there is some personal satisfaction . . . For I found my manhood sufficient for one of the hardest tests I've ever had: to "stand up in meeting" and say "no" to a steamroller . . .[10]

More than one steamroller was loose in the world, and the prospects in early 1950 for an agreement on nuclear weapons control had not exactly improved since the Soviet rejection of the Baruch Plan some three years before. Stalin's tyranny was still at its zenith; struggle was the hallmark of international life; the name for the times was cold war; and arms were the prime symbols of competitive pursuit of national interests presumed to be in conflict. The Communist parties of Western Europe, little more than branches of the Russian party, announced they would greet the arrival of the Red Army as a liberating force and meanwhile worked furiously to sabotage the Marshall Plan.

According to a subsequent account written in 1968 for *Science* magazine by Kapitza and a Russian colleague, the Russians began an all-out H-bomb project within two weeks of their first successful A-test and were well into it before the debate about the Super was foreclosed finally in Washington. And while the U.S. later produced the first "thermonuclear reaction," the Soviets produced the first operable thermonuclear bomb.

As Hans Bethe said in 1953 in the course of the Oppenheimer hearing, "I think maybe the suggestion to negotiate

again was one of desperation." [11] And Oppenheimer, on
the same occasion, said:

> The notion that the thermonuclear arms race was something
> that was in the interests of this country to avoid if it could
> was very clear to us in 1949 . . .
> This is an idea which I believe is still right, but I think that
> what was not clear to us then and what is clearer to me now is
> that it probably lay wholly beyond our power to prevent the
> Russians somehow from getting ahead with it . . .[12]

At the time, however, the conflict between secret decision-
making and the ways of the open society only became more
intense than ever for Oppenheimer. Shortly after the decision
to go for the Super, he appeared as a guest on a weekly radio
program conducted by Eleanor Roosevelt; and in the course
of it he said:

> The decision to seek or not to seek international control of
> atomic energy, the decision to try to make or not to make the
> hydrogen bomb, these are complex technical things, but they
> touch the very base of our morality. It is a grave danger for us
> that these decisions are taken on the basis of facts held secret.
> This is not because those who contributed to the decisions or
> make them are lacking in wisdom; it is because wisdom itself
> cannot flourish and even the truth not be established, without
> the give and take of debate and criticism. The facts, the rele-
> vant facts, are of little use to an enemy, yet they are funda-
> mental to an understanding of the issues of policy. If we are
> guided by fear alone, we will fail in this time of crisis. The
> answer to fear can't always lie in the dissipation of its cause;
> sometimes it lies in courage.[13]

12

Paranoia and Other Pleasantries: Two Schools of Security Doctrine

THE PERIOD from early 1950 to mid-1953 was a complex one for national security policy, military strategy, and nuclear affairs in the United States.

A presidential decision had been made to go all out to try to beat the Russians to the draw with the thermonuclear bomb; Congress passed large deficiency appropriation bills to finance the effort; the number of scientists and engineers working on the fusion problem at Los Alamos jumped from perhaps half a dozen to several hundred; and the General Advisory Committee of the AEC worked out a large expansion program for production of fissionable materials in anticipation of the new weapon, incorporating a design idea of Oppenheimer's which would make it possible for the new facilities to produce materials either for nuclear or thermonuclear reactions.

In short, the decision was made and the resources were available; yet the ideas were not. For more than a year the news about the Super project would be all bad. The theoretical model on which Teller and his associates had been working looked less and less feasible. New calculations at Los Alamos led to the conclusion that even if a thermonuclear explosion could be made to work, it could not be built into a deliverable weapon and would, in any event, have such an enormous appetite for fissionable materials as to all but devour the rest of the nuclear program.

As Air Force Major General James McCormack, Jr., director of the Division of Military Application of the AEC during the period when the H-bomb decision was made, said in the course of the Oppenheimer hearings, ". . . I am not aware of any delays in the thermonuclear program that occurred for any reason other than just not knowing how to do the next step . . ." [1]

In any case, in the spring of 1950, shortly after the President's announcement of intention to pursue the Super bomb, Oppenheimer was called in to work on a National Security Council study of the impact of Soviet accession to atomic power; in effect, this was the "strategic reappraisal" that Acheson and Lilienthal had recommended. The study, of course, has not been made public; but Walter Millis says in *Arms and the State* that "in general it analyzed the new world situation and called for large expansions of our military, diplomatic, and economic effort in meeting it." [2] Oppenheimer said in the course of the hearings that "I approved and helped with some parts" of the study and that "I was very aware of the fact that you couldn't, within the atomic energy field alone, find a complete or even a very adequate answer to the Russian breaking of our monopoly." [3]

Whatever the Security Council paper recommended in the way of nonnuclear support of the national defense, the find-

ings would soon have a ready market; for the crash project
to build a super nuclear bomb in the United States was barely
six months old when war broke out in the Far East.

At its inception the Korean War seemed to be a traditional
war in most important respects. It began at a specific time
in a specific place with an armed attack by conventional forces
across a border; its purpose was military conquest; and the
weapons were familiar to prenuclear times. But, while the
story of the Korean War itself is not relevant to the present
recital, the Korean affair was in fact astonishingly nontradi-
tional in light of the long history of conquest by arms.

On the aggressor's side, it was a war by proxy — the Soviet
embassy in Pyongyang being in charge of North Korea at the
time.

On the defender's side, it was a military action sanctioned
by resolution of the United Nations and conducted under its flag, the Soviet Union incredibly having absented itself for long enough to permit the Security Council to de-
clare North Korea an aggressor under the terms of the United
Nations Charter.

Despite the atomic age, battles in Korea turned as before
on the fortunes of foot soldiers armed with rifles, machine
guns, and hand grenades, fighting for bloody little bits of
high ground like Porkchop Hill and Heartbreak Ridge. For
the Great Weapon, the targets were too small; besides, there
were political inhibitions against using them.

In the end — despite General MacArthur's nostalgic maxim
that there is "no substitute for victory" — the war ended
where it began, on the 38th parallel. There were some six
million casualties, military and civilian on both sides, but
only the merest speck of real estate changed hands. Neither

side defeated the other's army nor destroyed his will to wage war; peace negotiations and military battles were conducted simultaneously for more than a year; no swords were exchanged at the end of hostilities; and though fighting stopped eventually, there was no peace settlement to take its place.

From the UN side, the Korean War was a limited war fought for the limited objective of denying aggression in violation of an international compact, not for "victory," as in the past, and not at all in line with strategic bombing doctrine.

The world was not ready to adapt politically to the atomic revolution; but it still had the political option of leaving the revolutionary weapons unused in their arsenals. The only alternative to world government in the nuclear age might not, after all, be nuclear war.

Meanwhile, the U.S. military budget was doubled, the U.S. economy was semimobilized, and the U.S. armed services were confronted with a historic bit of irony: overwhelming superiority in destructive power proved unusable on a field of battle.

According to Oppenheimer, the Korean War led the General Advisory Committee of the AEC to spend most of its time worrying about the problem of "using an atomic explosive not merely in a strategic campaign but also in a defensive or tactical campaign." [4] Part of the problem, he said, was that of "adapting atomic warheads so that they could be used by a variety of carriers. This sometimes meant developing designs which were not, from the point of view of nuclear physics, the most perfect design, because you had to make a compromise in order to get the thing light or small or thin or whatever else it was that the carrier required . . ." [5]

This, of course, was the direction in which Oppenheimer had been urging the AEC and the military services to proceed for some time. Among those impressed with the point that conventional military forces were not yet obsolete was, not surprisingly, General Maxwell D. Taylor, commander of the Eighth Army in Korea. Shortly after the armistice, he wrote to his chief of staff, General Matthew Ridgway:

> An outstanding impression from the operations in Korea has been the ineffectiveness or inapplicability of many of our modern weapons to the requirements of the Korean type of limited war . . . The enemy, terrain, and weather combined to nullify in a large measure much of the costly equipment assembled during and after World War II in preparation for a possible World War III, to be fought principally in Western Europe. To these restrictions we added the subjective factor of our own reluctance to use atomic and other special weapons in which we have been investing a large part of the military budget.
>
> The absence of an opponent prevented the useful employment of much of our air and naval strength . . . at sea the mightiest warships of the world were obliged to occupy themselves with shelling relatively unimportant targets ashore, or to maintaining a blockade against negligible enemy naval forces.
>
> Finally, we denied ourselves the use of special weapons (i.e. atomic weapons) for a variety of reasons, some military, some political . . . Regardless of the merits of the case for and against the use of special weapons in Korea, the fact that we deliberately abstained from using them is a reminder that we may do so again in future situations, particularly as the Soviet atomic capability increases.

To this General Taylor juxtaposed a startling bit of prophesy: "In the end, by a tacitly agreed, mutual cancelling out of special weapons, we may be forced to rely again on conventional means." [6] The commander of the Eighth Army and Robert Oppenheimer seemed to be on the same wave length: the United States should be prepared for "more than one kind of war."

Oppenheimer still felt he should resign from the General Advisory Committee because of his recommendation against the Super. As he said in the hearing, "I felt a little uncomfortable about continuing in that office." Lilienthal had resigned from the AEC for private life and had been succeeded by Gordon Dean, and there were other changes around the commission. In the fall of 1950, a few months after the start of the Korean War, Oppenheimer discussed what he called "this obvious personal worry" with Chairman Dean and Commissioner Henry Smyth. But "they protested in very forceful terms that I should not quit as chairman, and that they would be very unhappy if I did . . . that I ought to carry on." Oppenheimer then raised the question of resignation with the advisory committee but found, as he related it in the hearings, that "our committee was not a very responsive group when it came to electing other chairmen and I got no place . . ." [7]

So Oppenheimer stayed on at his various government posts. As chairman of the General Advisory Committee, he was responsible for helping out in the continuing search for the Super bomb. It was not going well, but Oppenheimer was reluctant to have the advisory committee report pessimistically about a project it had opposed in the first instance. He and other members visited Los Alamos for seminars with Teller and the other scientists, reviewed the state of the art, offered what advice they could, and then passed on to the AEC commissioners, without further comment, transcripts of these discouraging reviews.

In his other capacities, Oppenheimer was involved mainly in the general reappraisal of atomic weaponry sparked by the Korean conflict. At the end of 1950, about the time the Chinese Communists entered the war in Korea, and while the Super project was still on dead center, Oppenheimer chaired a six-day meeting of the Committee on Atomic Energy of the Research and Development Board of the Defense Department. It was a mixed military-civilian group; General Wilson was among the officers and Dr. Alvarez among the civilians. As Alvarez recalled it, Oppenheimer asked him to serve because, "I know you represent a viewpoint different from mine, and I think it would be healthy to have you on this committee." [8]

As Oppenheimer recalled that meeting in the course of the hearings, it was a time of

. . . alerts about the possibility of attack on the continental United States, a time of very great anxiety. We addressed ourselves to the question with what we have [in the way of nuclear arms] and can have soon, how rapidly we can get a really effective use of the atomic capability that we have developed. What can we do fast about this . . . It was also a time at which technical prospects of the thermonuclear program were quite bleak. We so reported . . . I think it is interesting that there was no difference of opinion among us . . . [9]

What the committee recommended that "could be done fast about this" was not made public. But Dr. Marvin Kelly, a member of the group, recalled receiving a letter of appreciation for the work of the committee stating that its report had been "accepted favorably in both the AEC Commission and the military." He added that ". . . I know from my participation in the [atomic energy] program that what happened in the succeeding years was very much along the line or substantially identical to the charter that we suggested . . ."

The general lines of those recommendations were indicated by Dr. Kelly when he said:

> This was just at the threshold of the time where atomic basic knowledge had reached the point that it was possible to consider versatility. By that I mean extending the range of weapons well beyond that of the large free-falling bombs . . .
>
> That opportunity for extending the scope of weapons, that is the range of versatility in military action, was a thing that needed very careful weighing — and was weighed — and our report encompassed the views on how that should be broadened . . .[10]

"Throughout this," Dr. Kelly testified, "Dr. Oppenheimer was one of us in views . . . as to the best military use of the fissionable materials and the kind of weapons that should be put into development . . ." After the panel completed its work, Oppenheimer prepared a report which was approved by the panel and submitted in January 1951.

It was during this period that the military agencies increasingly adopted the practice of awarding contracts to universities and "think tanks" to conduct studies bearing on the immensely more complex military problems of the atomic age. These too would absorb the time and attention of Oppenheimer who, in the process, became not just a direct consultant to the government but a consultant to consultants to the government.

The Massachusetts Institute of Technology, for example, was asked to consider the problem of air defense — an exercise code-named Project Charles — which in turn led to the establishment of the Lincoln Laboratory, a large radar and air defense research center operated by MIT for the armed services under a contract from the Air Force.

Oppenheimer, though he played a minor role in Project Charles, was consulted in the process. More importantly, he served on the advisory council of a study project which he himself had suggested on the problems of civil defense. It was code-named East River and directed by Dr. Lloyd Berkner, president of Associated Universities. Rabi and Lauritsen were active on the project and Oppenheimer concurred with the general finding of this group to the effect that ". . . if civil defense was to be manageable at all, early warning and improved military interception, improved over what we then had or were planning, were an essential part of making civil defense manageable . . ." [11]

Meanwhile, in the spring of 1951, a sudden break came in the search for the Super —at least from a theoretical point of view. It occurred in the course of a meeting at Princeton, convened by Oppenheimer to review the status of fusion research. The five AEC commissioners and their general manager were there; the Weapons Subcommittee of the General Advisory Committee was there; the director of the Los Alamos Laboratory, Dr. Norris Bradbury, was there; and so were Dr. Teller and other nuclear physicists invited to participate. Oppenheimer was chairman.

When Teller came to the Princeton meeting he had a completely new theoretical approach to a hydrogen bomb — in his head. Teller said later, in the course of the Oppenheimer hearings, that he had approached the Princeton meeting "with considerable misgivings, because I expected that the General Advisory Committee, and particularly Dr. Oppenheimer, would further oppose the development." [12] As things turned out, Teller's premonitions were without foundation. As he began to expound the new ideas and to write out formulas on a blackboard, others suddenly caught fire. Fermi, Bethe, Oppenheimer, and others jumped into the discussion.

More calculations were chalked on the blackboard and the group was seized with the exciting sense of being on the edge of discovery. It was one of those unpredictable things: Teller, after puzzling about nuclear fusion for eleven years, at last had hold of something that might work; the tension was reminiscent of Göttingen and Los Alamos. The Princeton meeting went on for another two days and when it was over Oppenheimer had concluded that "the theory was beautiful and the technology was sweet." As Teller said in the course of the hearings:

> . . . Dr. Oppenheimer warmly supported this new approach and I understand he made a statement to the effect that if anything of this kind had been suggested right away he never would have opposed it. [13]

AEC Chairman Dean was enthusiastic too:

> At the end of those two days we were all convinced, everyone in the room, that at least we had something for the first time that looked feasible in the way of an idea — everyone around that table . . . was enthusiastic now you had something foreseeable . . . The bickering was gone. The discussions were pretty well ended . . . [14]

Or so it seemed to Dean in the spring of 1951. That summer, Bethe reversed his earlier decision and returned to Los Alamos to work with Teller on the H-bomb. As for Oppenheimer, there would be, toward the end of the summer, another study project to lay claim on his time.

This one was known as Project Vista, entrusted by the Army to the California Institute of Technology at Pasadena. Testimony about the Vista Project in the course of the Oppenheimer hearing is heavily censored; the whole scope of the inquiry is not known publicly. It is clear, however, that Chapter Five of the ultimate report had to do with the use of nuclear weapons by ground forces for defense against large-scale aggression — that is, the tactical use of nuclear weapons, especially for the defense of Western Europe. There were no such weapons available for Europe at the time; nor had tactics yet been developed for the use of atomic arms in a land battle.

It is clear, too, how Oppenheimer approached the Vista Project, for he said in the course of the hearings:

. . . When the war ended the United States had a weapon which revolutionized strategic air warfare . . . The Air Force went hard to work to make best possible use of it . . . The bomb that was developed and embellished in the years 1945 to 1948, and the aircraft that go with it, the whole weapons system, can of course be used on any target, but it is a very inappropriate one for a combat theatre. Therefore there was the problem of developing the weapon, the weapons system, the tactics to give a new capability which would be as appropriate as possible under fire, and in the combat theatre . . . It was simply another job that needed doing, and which . . . ought not to be competitive [with strategic bombing requirements] any more than continental defense is, which is another part of the defense of the country and of the free world . . .[15]

Oppenheimer did not join the project at Pasadena until the fall. By that time, drafts of various chapters for the emerging study were in preparation. For one thing, a draft of Chapter Five had been prepared by Bacher, Lauritsen, and several other members of the project. Bacher and others testified that when Oppenheimer reviewed the draft of Chapter Five, he had some ideas about how to rearrange the material and improve the presentation of the recommendations. He either rewrote the chapter or wrote a new summary of it and, in the process, became identified as the "author" of Chapter Five of the Vista Report: it was a credit he could have done without.

The content of that chapter alarmed the Air Force representatives at Pasadena, especially David Griggs. Griggs at the time held the title of Chief Scientist of the Air Force, though he commented in the course of the Oppenheimer hearings that the title "doesn't mean anything." In any case, Griggs had been a consultant to the Rand Corporation engaged primarily in research work for the Air Force, while working as a professor of geophysics at the University of California before coming to Washington as "chief scientist" to the Air Force. Griggs later testified during the Oppenheimer hearings as to what bothered him about the Vista Project as it began to shape up: "There were three things about the Vista Report that I regarded as unfortunate from the standpoint of the Air Force," [16] he said.

Exactly what those three things were is a bit obscured in the censored transcript. It is plain from the testimony, however, that they had to do with the specific types of weapons — strategic and tactical — that should be accumulated in the nuclear arsenal; with the allocation of fissionable materials

to categories of weapons; and with a judgment about the
state of knowledge with respect to the thermonuclear bomb.
As Griggs recalled it, the draft Vista Report included a
"statement to the effect that in the state of the art it
was impossible to assess the capabilities of thermonuclear
weapons adequately to evaluate their tactical significance" [16]
— despite the fact that, as Griggs said, "Dr. Teller had
visited the Vista Project not very long before this, and had
attempted to persuade the Vista people that a thermonuclear
weapon was in such a state that it should be included in
studies . . . of atomic warfare." [17]

Griggs said he believed that at least two of the three ob-
jectionable points were in a short introduction to Chapter
Five and he had been told that Oppenheimer had drafted
the introduction. Even if Oppenheimer didn't invent the
points, Griggs said he was fairly sure that he "approved"
them or at least was "aware" of them.

On cross-examination, Griggs was asked whether the disputed part of the Vista Report contained "a recommendation
that we should be prepared with some degree of flexibility
to be able to use either strategic or tactical airpower, which-
ever or both might be desirable in the light of the circum-
stances which might arise." Griggs replied that he was "quite
sure it contained strong emphasis on the desirability for
flexibility in the use of atomic weapons." [18]

Despite the censorship, the thrust of Chapter Five also
was clear from the testimony of Lauritsen: "We were advocating," he said, "the development and use of weapons that
would be suitable for precise delivery at close range from our
troops and in all kinds of weather . . ." This, he said, was
essential "to destroy mass attacks like we have seen in World

War II so often on the Russsian front, and like we have seen in Korea. To hold, it was necessary to have atomic weapons that could be delivered on short notice, with high accuracy . . . We felt that with the growing stockpile it was wise and besides, that it was necessary . . ."

From the viewpoint of the Strategic Air Command something far more sinister was implied in what Lauritsen added to his testimony:

> . . . we felt it was wise to use part of our stockpile [of fissionable material] or to divide part of the stockpile so that it could be used for this purpose [tactical nuclear weapons] if necessary . . . we felt that . . . it would not be wise to devote all of our stockpile to strategic weapons.[19]

Years later Robert McNamara would point out: ". . . a strategic planner must be conservative in his calculations; that is, he must prepare for the worst plausible case . . ."[20] Whatever the stockpile of nuclear bombs might have been at the beginning of the 1950s, it was unlikely that the Strategic Air Command would have considered it adequate to its needs in the event of total war with the Soviet Union. It could therefore follow that any proposal that diverted resources away from the most rapid accumulation of the maximum number of the largest strategic nuclear weapons could be taken as a proposal contrary to the national security interests of the United States.

One could even come to doubt the motivations of anyone who advanced or supported such proposals. As Griggs would say in the course of the Oppenheimer hearings:

> I have been involved in . . . a number of pretty strong controversies in the military, and it is a fair general observation

that when you get involved in a hot enough controversy, it is awfully hard not to question the motives of people who oppose you.[21]

This was the lethal virus that began to infect the national security community between 1950 and 1953. There was a gradual polarization into two camps: the short war and Big Bomb men on the one hand, and those in favor of also being prepared for a flexible response to violence at lesser levels on the other. It was never quite an either-or proposition with one group or the other; it was more a matter of relative importance, of priority of effort. But priorities settle the allocation of budgetary and other resources and determine schedules which advance or retard deadlines for the achievement of goals. And so the basis for controversy was inherent in the question even of the relative emphasis placed on nuclear versus conventional arms, or on larger versus smaller nuclear bombs, or on offensive versus defensive systems. Even to lean one way or the other raised the issue of the unlimited versus limited warfare doctrine.

Oppenheimer consistently was on the opposite side of the "hot controversies" from Griggs and some others. For example, there was the argument over whether a new laboratory should be created under Teller to take the work on the hydrogen bomb away from Los Alamos, where Teller was having trouble getting along with some of his colleagues. Months after the breakthrough meeting at Princeton in the spring of 1951, the project simply did not seem to be going forward. In the course of the hearings, Oppenheimer recalled that after a review of the problems with Teller in Chicago during the autumn of that year, intervening work on the Super had "only made things look tied together."

It was on this occasion, Oppenheimer remembered, that Teller told him that he had no confidence in some of the people responsible for the H-bomb development at Los Alamos and "he expressed to me the view that Fermi or Bethe or I would be the only people that he would be happy to work with."

Fermi and Bethe already had declined, and the idea of returning full-time to Los Alamos was an awkward and unwelcome one to Oppenheimer; but he said "it would depend on whether I would be welcomed by Bradbury . . . It seemed to me a bad thing for an ex-director to return . . . I don't believe that it would have been practical . . . I would have been ancient and not on my toes anymore, and I doubt if I would have felt appropriate . . ." [22]

Nonetheless Oppenheimer did telephone Bradbury to report his conversation with Teller and, as Oppenheimer said in the course of the hearings: ". . . he gave no signs of wanting the ex-director back, and said he had full confidence in the present man, and that was that."

On several occasions, Oppenheimer recommended other physicists for recruitment by Teller and held open an appointment to the Institute for Advanced Study so that a scientist whom Teller particularly wanted to help him could go to Los Alamos instead. Teller acknowledged in the course of the hearings that Oppenheimer had been "exceedingly cooperative" in this regard.

But Teller and the Air Force officials were increasingly frustrated by the lack of progress on the Super, and they began to focus the blame on the Los Alamos laboratory, the General Advisory Committee, and on the person of Robert Oppenheimer.

In the course of the Oppenheimer hearing DuBridge was asked about a luncheon meeting at a private home in Washington to which he and Rabi were invited along with Griggs and at which Griggs, according to DuBridge, "disagreed with Dr. Rabi and myself very violently on some points." For one thing, "Griggs made what we considered to be false statements, that the GAC had impeded thermonuclear development." Rabi and DuBridge argued the contrary case.

The discussion apparently went to deeper questions of strategy and policy. Counsel for the AEC at the hearing had in hand a top secret paper which seemed to be a memorandum of the luncheon conversation. DuBridge was asked if he recalled Rabi's commenting to the effect that more important than the H-bomb was "a concerted effort of the best minds in this country toward peace with Soviet Russia" and that Oppenheimer, Lauritsen, and Rabi would "press for action" with the State Department along such lines.

DuBridge did not remember the point but said he thought Rabi probably felt at the time that "because of the terrifying implications of H-bombs and thermonuclear weapons, it was desirable to make another attempt to find a way to avoid using them." In general he said of their "very vigorous discussion" with Griggs:

> Our difference of point of view with Mr. Griggs, as I recall, was that he felt that the thermonuclear weapon development and production was No. 1 priority for the country. We felt that improving our fission weapon program and improving our defense were just as important, if not more important, at that time.[23]

As a result of these differences a campaign was launched for the Air Force to start its own laboratory devoted to the search for the H-bomb, with Teller in charge. The Air Force began preliminary negotiations with the University of Chicago, where Teller was on the faculty, for management of a new Air Force weapons laboratory. As Oppenheimer said in the course of the hearings:

At that time, Teller's unhappiness with the arrangements became quite generally known, and we were frequently asked by the Commission, "Should there be a second laboratory?" We were asked "Should this work be split off in some way from Los Alamos?"

I think, on this point, we were not unanimous. I think Dr. Libby [Dr. Willard Libby, then a member of the General Advisory Committee] thought it would be a good idea to have a second laboratory at any time . . . the purpose . . . would be to house Teller and bring young people into the program who were not now working on it, even though this might take some people away from Los Alamos, even though it might interfere with the work then going on. The rest of us, I think, were fairly clear that things were really going along marvelously well . . .

In any case, during the winter, our recommendations were to fix up Los Alamos so that it could do the job rather than start a separate establishment . . .[24]

Rabi also was asked in the course of the Oppenheimer hearings about the "second laboratory" issue. "That question came up again and again," he said. "Los Alamos is an awkward place and so on, and people kept on saying . . . that competition is good. Los Alamos has been criticized for being too conservative and stodgy. The suggestion that some other group utilizing talent which for some reason or another was unobtainable at Los Alamos would be a good thing.

I, myself . . . was not in favor of that and my own reason
was . . . that Los Alamos was a miracle of a laboratory . . .
just a miracle of a place.

. . . So my own feeling was, they are doing remarkably well
and why upset the applecart . . .[25]

The matter also came up in the testimony of Bethe, who
had paid a call on Griggs in the spring of 1952.
"At the time," Bethe said:

there was much discussion of the past record of Los Alamos and
much discussion of the question whether a second laboratory
for weapons work should be opened. It seemed to me that some
rather false information was current with some people, particularly in the Air Force, and one of the persons whom I knew
to be an exponent of this section of Air Force opinion was
Dr. Griggs. Therefore, I went to see him to clear up the past
Los Alamos record, and also to discuss generally the function of
thermonuclear weapons in warfare . . .

. . . It was believed by Dr. Oppenheimer and myself and by
the members of the Atomic Energy Commission that Los Alamos was doing a very good job at that time . . .

Dr. Teller, I think, was conducting a campaign to establish
the contrary . . .

Dr. Griggs had been very much an exponent of the view that
Los Alamos was not doing its job right and . . . of the view
that thermonuclear weapons and only the biggest thermonuclear weapons should be the main part of the weapons arsenal of the United States . . .[26]

In due course a compromise was reached. The Livermore
Laboratory at Berkeley, which had worked mainly on in-
strumentation for nuclear weapons tests, was expanded to
supplement the work of Los Alamos on thermonuclear weapons. E. O. Lawrence was in overall charge of atomic work

for the University of California; Dr. Herbert York was made director of Livermore; and Teller became head scientist and idea man. This arrangement was approved by the General Advisory Committee because of the existing managerial framework of the University of California, because it did not threaten the work program or morale at Los Alamos, and because it provided a place where Teller could bring his high talents to bear in harmonious relationship with Lawrence.

The issue of the "second laboratory" was more than a jurisdictional quarrel or a problem in the administration of a scientific enterprise; it was further evidence of the festering division between two schools of thought on national security. The two laboratories symbolized the competition revealed gently by Bethe at the end of his testimony about the events leading to the establishment of Livermore. "This laboratory," he said, "has been getting all the credit for thermonuclear development, which is unjustified." Asked to explain that comment, he said, "I mean . . . that the majority of the weapons which have been developed, and which are being tested now [1954] in the Pacific, and the most powerful of them, were developed exclusively by the Los Alamos Laboratory." [27]

Rabi put it a bit more strongly: "I think in popular opinion such as *Time* magazine, and so on, it is that laboratory [Livermore] which produced the thermonuclear weapon. That is a lie." [28]

Teller himself seemed to confirm the point when he volunteered during the Oppenheimer hearings: "Livermore laboratory is a very new laboratory and I think it is doing a very nice job, but published reports about its importance have been grossly and embarrassingly exaggerated." [29]

The controversy over the "second laboratory" was hardly patched up on the surface before a new project was under way which would deepen the split. This was the so-called Lincoln Summer Study, conducted at the Lincoln Laboratory at MIT in the summer of 1952.

Dr. Albert G. Hill, professor of physics at MIT and director of the laboratory, formulated the idea of the summer study with Dr. Jerrold Zacharias, also a physics professor at MIT and an associate director of the laboratory. One of the chief objectives was to follow up on the conclusion of Project East River and determine whether an early warning system could be contrived for the defense of the North Atlantic continent, a question that they had been discussing from time to time with Berkner. They also discussed the idea with Rabi, Lauritsen, and Oppenheimer — the latter because, as Zacharias said in the hearings, "his head is so clear . . . that when you flounder for months to try to formulate your ideas, you get to him and he can listen and help state clearly what you and he and others have decided is the germ of what you are thinking . . ." [30]

Also the organizers of the summer study proposal wanted the prestige of the Oppenheimer name to help attract other talent to the project. After discussing it among themselves, Zacharias agreed to serve as director of the study, Lauritsen agreed to work on it, and Oppenheimer and Rabi agreed to serve part-time and to allow the use of their names.

Oppenheimer's interest in the Lincoln project is clear from his testimony about the prospects for intercepting an incoming air attack at that time:

. . . In the Spring of 1952, the official views of what we could do were extremely depressing . . . and there were methods of attack which appeared to be quite open to the enemy where it was doubtful that we would either detect or intercept any substantial fraction of the aircraft at all.

My view is that this was by no means a happy situation at all, and I know of no reason to think that it ever will be a happy situation, but that the steps that are now [1954] being taken and others that will come along as technology develops are immensely worth taking if they only save some American lives, if they only preserve some American cities, and if they only create in the planning of the enemy some doubt as to the effectiveness of their strikes . . . [31]

On the same occasion Zacharias explained the purpose of the summer study:

The purpose of the summer study was simply this. We knew that the Russian threat might grow in a variety of ways. The types of aircraft, the types of delivery means, including ballistic missiles and so on, would increase, and we wanted to see whether the kind of air defense work going on within Lincoln was appropriate to the growing threat . . .[32]

"Remember," Zacharias said, "that this was a time when the early warning for the Air Force against incoming raids was pitifully short in time. Substantially no warning until enemy bombers might be directly on us. We therefore wanted to look at the early warning, the air battles, and possibilities of defense against new types . . . of delivery. This was our objective." [33]

Zacharias insisted that there was no conflict between a strong strategic striking force and a strong continental defense system, that in fact they are both part of a single concept of security. As he explained it:

. . . it is clear to anyone who tries to think of the defense of the continent . . . that there are essentially . . . four possible rings of defense. One is an innermost last-ditch affair, largely from the ground with the aid of missiles or antiaircraft guns; a second ring which can be provided by interceptor aircraft of short range and moderately close to home; a third ring which is farther out away from our shores . . . ; and a fourth which is the destruction of enemy bases by means of long-range bombardment aircraft. All of these elements for defense of the continent are terribly important . . .[34]

Nor did Oppenheimer see a contradiction between continental defense and a strategic strike force — any more than he saw a contradiction between conventional and nuclear armaments. When he testified about the Lincoln Summer Study he said:

First, strategic airpower is one of the most important ingredients of continental defense. Both with the battle of Europe and with the intercontinental battle, clearly the best place to destroy aircraft is on enemy fields, and that is a job for strategic airpower.

Second, at least the warning elements and many of the defensive elements of continental defense are needed to protect the bases, the aircraft, which take part in the strategic air campaign. This is the two-way relation . . .[35]

But the Lincoln Summer Study had trouble getting started. Griggs had certain concerns about the project which he referred to in the course of the Oppenheimer hearings:[36] "There was perhaps too much emphasis assigned to the development of an early warning line across our northernmost approaches . . ." Interest in this possibility had been stimulated by "the rather exciting new . . . technological developments in this field, which had been brought forward . . . principally by Dr. Lloyd Berkner." This worried Griggs because it suggested a "Maginot Line type of concept."

Griggs also testified that "one of the things we were afraid of was that the Lincoln Summer Study might get out of hand, from our [Air Force] standpoint, in the sense that they might be reported directly to higher authority, such as the National Security Council."

He said he was "upset" at the idea that the study might consider "the relative role of the Strategic Air Command and the Air Defense Command," adding that ". . . we have learned to be a little cautious about study projects which have in mind making budget allocations or recommending budget allocations for major components of the Military Establishment . . ." The people engaged in the Lincoln Summer Study, like those in the Vista Project, were not, he said, "charged with the responsibility of . . . the activities of the Strategic Air Command."

Griggs professed fear that bringing well-known outside talent into the Air Force-controlled laboratory for an ad hoc project might distract the attention of the regular staff; and the one piece of outside talent to which he specifically objected was Robert Oppenheimer. As he explained this in the course of the hearing:

> It became apparent to us . . . that there was a pattern of activities all of which involved Dr. Oppenheimer . . . Of these one was . . . his activity in the Vista Project . . . We were told in the late Fall, I believe, of 1950, that Oppenheimer and two other colleagues formed an informal committee of three to work for world peace or some such purpose . . . We were also told that . . . they considered that many more things were

more important than the development of the thermonuclear weapons, specifically the air defense of the continental United States, which was the subject of the Lincoln Summer Study . . .

Additional testimony by Griggs and by Rabi and Lauritsen strongly suggests that Griggs got these impressions in the course of his luncheon argument with them about the proposed second laboratory. On that occasion, Rabi and Lauritsen said that agreement with Russia — and even improved air defenses — were more important to U.S. security than the acquisition of H-bombs. They also said that they intended to press that view on Oppenheimer, which apparently accounts for Griggs's "informal committee of three to work for world peace or some such purpose."

"It was further told me," Griggs continued in his testimony, "by people who were approached to join the summer study that in order to achieve world peaace . . . it was necessary not only to strengthen the air defense of the continental United States but also to give up something, and the thing that was recommended that we give up was . . . the strategic part of our total air power . . ." Under questioning, Griggs attributed this suggestion to Zacharias. Zacharias testified under oath in the hearing that no scientist connected with the project had any recommendation about the strategic air arm beyond the feeling that it should be strengthened.

Meanwhile some of the people who were approached to join the summer study were hearing something else about Oppenheimer. Dr. Hill testified that a civilian adviser to the Air Force came to him to express concern about Oppenheimer's participation "for security reasons," and added that "quite a few others mentioned that Griggs was talking about it and had talked to them." [37]

Griggs testified that he took his concerns to Air Force Secretary Finletter as a result of which "I was asked to inform him so that steps could be taken to correct this condition, or to cancel the summer study if that were necessary."

It appeared that Griggs felt that it might be necessary to somehow cancel the whole summer study project. As Hill said in the Oppenheimer hearings:

> He [Griggs] evidently was concerned that the purpose . . . was to come out with a master plan of how to divide money between the Strategic Air Command and the Air Defense Command. Such was farthest from our thoughts . . .
>
> I don't know where Griggs got this idea . . . I know for a while he was quite concerned about this summer study, and about allowing it to be set up . . .[38]

Zacharias was more emphatic:

> . . . as I saw it, he [Griggs] was doing everything he could to prevent our starting the summer study. He tried to influence people not to join it. He tried to influence President Killian and Provost Stratton [of MIT] to prevent the initiation of the summer study . . .
>
> Dr. Griggs' efforts — let me use a strong word — to sabotage the summer study from a position of power as chief scientist for the Air Force I regarded as unwise, but . . . I would not want to bring up Dr. Griggs on charges of being disloyal . . . However, let me say rather informally that it is a bit of a pity that duelling has gone out of style . . .
>
> . . . there are personal differences that are very strong . . .

in the old days some of these were settled by duelling . . .
having read some of Dr. Griggs' testimony, my blood begins to
boil a bit. I feel no great liking for Dr. Griggs at this particular
point.

Zacharias was then asked the straight question: "Do you
question Mr. Griggs' veracity?" The answer was: "Yes, I
would." [39]

Griggs and Oppenheimer were not unknown to each other
before the Lincoln Summer Study affair. In the course of
the luncheon argument with Rabi about the work of the
General Advisory Committee, Rabi had maintained that
Griggs could not understand the rationale of the GAC on the
Super issue without reading the minutes of the meeting. Toward the end of May 1952, Griggs called on Oppenheimer at
Princeton to see the paper in question. On June 21, he prepared the following memorandum, classified "Eyes Only"
for Finletter:

1. In view of your possible meeting with Oppenheimer I want
to record as accurately as I can my recollection of parts of my
conversation with him on May 23, 1952.
2. I said I had heard from associates of his a story, as follows:
"At one of the briefings given by Teller on the implications of
the H-bomb, a high official of the Department of Defense ex-
claimed 'If only we could have [censored] of those [H-bombs]
we could rule the world.'" Oppenheimer said that he was familiar with the story, said that it had occurred at the briefing
of Mr. Lovett.
I told him that I was present at that briefing, and that nothing could be farther from the actual reaction of those present.
He then stated that he had confidence in the reliability of his
information, and further, that it was "my boss" who is supposed to have said it. On further questioning, he left no doubt

in my mind that it was you to whom he was referring, although he did not use your name.

3. I have heard this story used by him and others as an illustration of the dangerous warmongers who rule the Pentagon and who are going to precipitate this Nation into a war unless a few scientists can save it.

4. After he had showed me the GAC recommendation of December 1949 that the United States not intensify H-bomb development, but publicly renounce its development, and when I was pressing the point that such a course of action could well be disastrous to this country, Oppenheimer asked if I thought he were pro-Russian or just confused. After a moment I replied frankly that I wish I knew. He then asked if I had "impugned his loyalty." I replied I had. He then said he thought I was paranoid. After a few more pleasantries our conversation came to an end.[40]

Paranoid or not, Griggs's fears about the Vista and Lincoln Summer Study projects turned out to be fantasies. In December 1951, three of the scientists who had worked on the Vista Project — Oppenheimer, DuBridge, and Lauritsen — accompanied Whitman to Paris where they discussed the draft Vista Report with General Eisenhower, then Supreme Commander, Allied Forces Europe. The recommendations for adapting tactical nuclear weapons to the support of defensive ground forces were welcomed by the commander of NATO troops facing superior conventional land and air forces of the Soviet Union and its satellites. After some adaptation, the Vista Report turned out to be acceptable to the Air Force as well.

Indeed, in the course of the Oppenheimer hearings, Griggs himself said that "the Vista Report was a very fine job and particularly in connection with the recommendations for the use of atomic weapons . . . and specifically, I think, it is quite appropriate to say that Dr. Oppenheimer's contribution in this direction was helpful to the Air Force . . . I am reasonably sure that some of the things I regarded as favorable in the Vista Report were in some measure at least the product of Mr. Oppenheimer's contribution." [41]

As for the Lincoln Summer Study, Oppenheimer was duly cleared for work on it. It began with a four-day technical briefing. Dr. Zacharias described the occasion in the Oppenheimer hearings:

> We had for the first week of that study a briefing . . . that was packed with as much meat as you can get into any four days of technical briefing. I wanted a summary of that technical briefing and there were about sixty-five people there, all very fully informed, and the only man I could turn to to give a summary, who could pull the thing together, was Dr. Oppenheimer. He did a masterful job . . .[42]

After that, Oppenheimer, who did not consider himself an expert on radar, attended sessions at the Lincoln Laboratory only from time to time. In due course the group came up with a report which endorsed the need for both a strong strategic striking force and a strong continental defense; the principal recommendation was for an early warning system of radar installations, to be established well out on the Arctic route for air attack against the continent. When it came to the Oppenheimer hearing, Griggs testified: "I believe that as a result of the Lincoln Summer Study our air defense is materially improved."

Before the summer study got under way Oppenheimer had announced his determination to resign from the General

Advisory Committee when his six-year term expired in the fall. In the spring of 1952 he called on Chairman Dean and told him of his decision. At the same time, Oppenheimer agreed to accept a one-year contract as one of a panel of outside advisers with full security clearance who could be called upon when the AEC felt the need for advice. Dean wrote promptly to Oppenheimer a letter which concluded:

> It is impossible for me to magnify the contribution which, as Chairman of this distinguished group, you have made to the Commission and the country. It has been a magnificent one and we of the Commission will be forever grateful to you. The period covered by your Chairmanship has been one in which this new agency needed very much the wisest possible guidance. This we have received and no one knows this better than myself.
>
> I am quite aware that there is no one who can adequately take your place, but your willingness to remain as a consultant to the Commission somewhat softens the blow of your departure from the GAC Councils.[43]

Oppenheimer's colleagues on the GAC seemed to share Dean's view. At the hearing, Rabi would testify:

> I must say that Dr. Oppenheimer as chairman . . . always conducted himself in such a way as to elicit the opinions of the members and to stimulate the discussion. He is not one of those chairmen who sort of takes it their privilege to hold the floor; the very opposite . . . When he reported to the Commission it was always a miracle to the other members on the committee how he could summarize three days of discussions and give the proper weight to the opinion of every member, the proper shade . . . It was a rather miraculous performance.[44]

Whitman only used different words to say the same thing:

> He was very careful to outline the problem and to see to it that we had authoritative presentations on the situation on which we were to give advice . . . he made it quite a point to assure the participation and the expression of views by all members of the committee, not to initially state his own views and try to coerce others to those views.
>
> I think we were . . . remarkably impressed by his ability to summarize the conclusions and the thinking of the committee in the presentation before the Commissioners . . .[45]

In making the same point, DuBridge indicated that for all his anxieties about the atomic age and the course of the nuclear arms race, Robert Oppenheimer had not lost his charisma:

> . . . he resigned or attempted to resign each year . . . the committee unanimously rejected his recommendation each year, and asked him to continue to serve as chairman. He was so naturally a leader of our group that it was impossible to imagine that he should not be in the chair. He was the leader . . . first because his knowledge of the atomic energy work was far more intimate than that of any other member of the committee . . . He was the natural leader because we respected his intelligence, his judgment, his personal attitude toward the work of the committee . . . He was a natural and respected and at times a loved leader of that group.
>
> At the same time I should emphasize that at no time did he dominate the group or did he suppress opinions that did not agree with his own. In fact, he encouraged a full and frank and free exchange of ideas throughout the full history of the committee. That is the reason we liked him as a leader, because though he did lead and stimulate and inform and help us in our decisions, he never dominated nor suppressed contrary or different opinions . . .[46]

The decision to resign from the GAC would not be the end of public service for Robert Oppenheimer — nor of his anxieties. He already was engaged in two enterprises which would carry over after his departure from the AEC, and carry over, too, into the Eisenhower administration.

He was a member of a panel appointed by the State Department in the spring of 1952 to review the prospects for arms limitation, an assignment which left him "somewhat puzzled as to whether there was any reality to the job we had been asked to assume but willing at least to listen." At the first meeting of the panel, Secretary Acheson had said that "he would like . . . any study of the regulation of armaments . . . similar to the Acheson-Lilienthal Report of many years before . . . we ought to see whether we did not have something to say and get it written down." [47]

The other ongoing assignment was as a member of the Science Advisory Committee to the Office of Defense Mobilization in the Executive Office, on which Oppenheimer had served since its organization in 1951, a group which had a rather desultory life until it was reactivated after the inauguration of President Eisenhower.

When the time came to leave the GAC, Oppenheimer had another "Dear Oppie" note from Chairman Dean which spoke once more of the progress that had been made in atomic energy and to say, among other things:

> I sincerely hope that some day, when the ills of the world are sufficiently diminished, the complete story of this progress can be told, so that the contribution of you and your colleagues may find its rightful place in the chronicle of our times. [48]

He also received a note from President Truman:

. . . you may take great pride in the fact that you have made a lasting and immensely valuable contribution to the national security and to atomic energy progress in this Nation. It is a source of real regret to me that the full story of the remarkable progress that has been made in atomic energy during these past six years, and in which you have played so large a role, cannot be publicly disclosed, for it would serve as the finest possible tribute to the contribution you have made.

I shall always be personally grateful for the time and energy you have so unselfishly devoted to the work of the General Advisory Committee, for the conscientious and rewarding way in which you have brought your great talents to bear upon the scientific problems of atomic energy development, and for the notable part you have played in securing for the atomic energy program the understanding cooperation of the scientific community.

You have served your country long and well, and I am gratified by the knowledge that your wise counsel will continue to be available to the Atomic Energy Commission on a consultant basis . . .[49]

As it turned out, the Atomic Energy Commission would scarcely avail itself of Oppenheimer's counsel at all.

13

From Doctrine to Dogma:
Massive Retaliation

Sometime during the summer of 1952, Dr. Vannevar Bush learned of a secret plan to test a thermonuclear device in the Pacific around the first of November. He sought out Elihu Root and several members of the State Department's Disarmament Panel on which he had been appointed to serve: John Dickey, president of Dartmouth; Joseph Johnson of the Carnegie Foundation; Allan Dulles; Robert Oppenheimer, and several others. Then he wrote down some thoughts in a memorandum, of which no copy was made, and set off for Washington to give the Secretary of State his own opinion about the scheduled test.

Bush's memorandum has not been made public, but during the Oppenheimer hearings he was clear enough about what his opinions were at the time:

> There were two primary reasons why I took action at that time, and went directly to the Secretary of State. There was scheduled a test which evidently was going to occur early in November. I felt that it was utterly improper — and I still think so — for that test to be . . . just before election, to con-

front an incoming President with an accomplished test for which he would carry the full responsibility thereafter. For that test marked our entry into a very disagreeable type of world.

In the second place, I felt strongly that that test ended the possibility of the only type of agreement that I thought was possible with Russia at that time, namely an agreement to make no more tests. For that kind of an agreement would have been self-policing in the sense that if it was violated, the violation would be immediately known. I think that we made a grave error in conducting that test at that time, and not attempting to make that type of simple agreement with Russia. I think history will show that was a turning point . . . that those who pushed that thing through to a conclusion without making that attempt have a great deal to answer for.[1]

As far as is known this was the last attempt to avert the birth of a thermonuclear age. Bush's proposal was reminiscent of the recommendations of the General Advisory Committee three years previously; of the Franck Report; and finally of Bohr's idea. Even if prospects for international control over atomic energy were nil, Bush argued that it should be easier to forgo a new weapon which neither side as yet possessed than to reduce inventories of existing weapons. An agreement with the Soviet Union should be sought, he said, to ban the testing of atomic bombs before either side could test a thermonuclear weapon. No inspection would be required to detect a violation.

But on November 1, 1952, the world's first thermonuclear reaction inaugurated yet another age in human affairs. The American "device" was a long way from a usable weapon; but the first Russian thermonuclear test, nine months later, was a true weapons test.

As Bush well knew, the advent of this "very disagreeable kind of world" meant, among other things:

1. That the second nuclear revolution had come only four years after the first.
2. That weapons with no inherent limitations to their destructive potential had become the new fact of nuclear life.
3. That the arithmetical margin of nuclear superiority would be measured henceforth in megatons.
4. That the built-in military disadvantages to the United States of a nuclear-armed world would be vastly increased.
5. That the advent of thermonuclear weapons would reinforce the action-reaction pattern which gave the nuclear arms race its internal dynamic.

Success in the Pacific meant, too, that the early advocates of a Super weapon like Teller, Lawrence, Alvarez, and Latimer, seemed to be vindicated in their quarrel with the "conservative and stodgy" group represented by the General Advisory Committee and especially by its chairman.

By this time Oppenheimer already had left the GAC, with thoughts of a full-time academic life. Eisenhower was President, with thoughts of balanced budgets and "fiscal responsibility" in the life of the federal government.

During the election campaign Eisenhower had promised a "New Look" for the United States defense establishment, and "security with solvency" for all. At the same time, his Secretary of State-to-be, John Foster Dulles, spoke of "rolling back communism" by "mobilizing the moral forces of the Free World."

Once the new administration was established in Washington, the New Look for the defense establishment was quickly foreshadowed. George M. Humphrey had become Secretary of the Treasury and was reputed to be the most influential man in the cabinet. He was doctrinally committed to the imperative virtue of balancing the national books. John Emmet Hughes, a special assistant and speech writer for President Eisenhower, has given us the flavor of Humphrey's thoughts about national priorities in his book *The Ordeal of Power*:

> . . . from the first weeks of Eisenhower's first term, the pattern of Humphrey's convictions was clear. Vigorously and bluntly, he enlivened almost every Cabinet session with little polemics on checking deficits, spoken as ardently as Dulles' exhortations on checking Communists. And Humphrey at times almost seemed to view the deficits as the more menacing of the two enemies. "To get real tax reductions," he warned one early Cabinet meeting, suddenly facing the prospect of a $5 billion deficit, "You *have* to get Korea *out of the way*. And after that you have to go on and do something more — figure out a *completely new* military posture . . . We have to cut *one-third* out of the budget and you can't do that just by eliminating waste. This means, wherever necessary, using a meat axe." [2]

The "completely new military posture" would be known as Massive Retaliation, a posture designed, as Secretary of Defense Charles E. Wilson would explain it, to maximize the Air Force and minimize the foot soldier. Not all foot soldiers were persuaded that it was so new; some years later, General Taylor would write in *The Uncertain Trumpet*, "The New Look was little more than the old air power dogma set forth in Madison Avenue trappings and now formally buttressed upon Massive Retaliation as the central strategic concept." [3]

To note the similarity was to miss a fundamental and melancholy difference. It was one thing when one of the military services subscribed to a theory of total war and quite another when the assumption of total war became the central strategic concept of official United States Government defense policy.

In terms of destruction per dollar expended, nuclear bombs are the cheapest of all weapons. The old air power doctrine converged with budgetary doctrine to produce a new national dogma: Massive Retaliation as the "formal buttress" of the national security of the United States.

This would mean a number of things. It would mean that the Korean experience would be brushed aside in favor of weaponry a thousand times more powerful than the "special weapons" which had proved unusable in battles for the high ground of the Korean peninsula; it was a case of Hiroshima to Heartbreak Ridge and back again.

It would mean that the United States would become so dependent upon nuclear weapons that in the event of a major conventional aggression, it would have to choose between inaction and starting a thermonuclear war.

It would mean that the Big Bomb cult had carried the day in the long debate over military strategy and henceforward would sit at the center of decision-making in defense policy. It would mean other things too: when contending doctrine becomes accepted dogma, dissent is turned into heresy.

While the New Look was still a slogan without a policy, Oppenheimer was involved in several assignments unrelated to his new post as consultant to the AEC. During and after the presidential campaign, he continued to work with the State Department advisory panel on disarmament. As he recalled it during the hearings:

> . . . We had a look at what we had been asked to look at. We went over the studies of past efforts at disarmament . . . It was very clear that you could not negotiate with the Russians much about anything and that nothing was harder to negotiate about than disarmament, and if you put these two things together it just was the bleakest picture in the world . . .

If the present looked bleak the future looked even grimmer. Of this, Oppenheimer said in the hearing:

> We took a look at the armament situation, getting some estimates of the growth of Russian capability and some estimates of our own as a measure for where they might be some time in the future . . . We became vividly and painfully aware of what an unregulated arms race would lead to in the course of . . . five or ten years . . .

In the end the disarmament panel made five recommendations to the State Department. Two of them were never made public. There is inconclusive evidence in the transcript of the hearings that the panel may have recommended new diplomatic efforts for a fresh approach to arms control negotiations, though when Oppenheimer referred to them in the course of the hearing, he said, "They are not very ingenious."

As for the other three recommendations, the first was that ". . . the people of this country be given a better understanding of the atomic arms race."

The second was that ". . . we attempt . . . to work more closely with our allies on problems having to do with the offensive and defensive aspects of large weapons."

And the third that ". . . we take further measures

for continental defense as a supplement to our striking capability." [4]

Not much in the way of disarmament there, but the points were old favorites with Oppenheimer. The report of the panel was submitted to the Eisenhower administration shortly after its inauguration in January 1953. According to Oppenheimer's testimony in the hearing, he was then asked by President Eisenhower to appear before the National Security Council "more or less as an advocate" of the findings of the advisory panel. "I presented the arguments," he said, "which are still persuasive to me, in favor of these three steps." [5]

The first proposal of the disarmament panel was pursued. After a staff review, the National Security Council recommended that the President make a major public speech on the facts of life in the thermonuclear age. C. D. Jackson, the President's special assistant on psychological warfare, was put in charge of what became known as Operation Candor. Draft followed draft for the proposed presidential address.

According to Robert Donovan in *Eisenhower*, "no one particularly liked them." And "the President," he wrote, "did not wish to be in a position merely of horrifying the American people or of horrifying the Russian people. He wanted to tell the world of the awful consequences of nuclear warfare, but he did not want to leave the matter at that dead end," [6] which is to say the new President could see no way out of the old trap. It was to say, too, that there would be no informed public debate of the issues and dilemmas of conventional doctrines in the nuclear age.

While the disarmament panel was still engaged in its work, Oppenheimer also met with the Science Advisory Committee of the Office of Defense Mobilization to consider what recommendations the group could make to the new administration. Oppenheimer testified that "I think we concluded that we had been of no great use and as constituted and conceived we should be dissolved."

Before disbanding, the committee agreed on "some changes in research development in the Defense Department" that it wanted to recommend and, according to Oppenheimer's testimony: "We also said that somehow or other the Security Council might need and should certainly have available to it technical advice of the highest order and must have access to the whole community of science . . ." That was just the sort of thing that had worried Griggs about the Lincoln Summer Study: a group of scientists might report directly to "higher authority, such as the National Security Council," without prior clearance from the Air Force.

DuBridge, chairman of the advisory committee to the Office of Defense Mobilization, went with Oppenheimer to see Nelson Rockefeller, who had been put in charge of a group studying the reorganization of the Executive Branch for the new administration. "We talked a good bit about our good-for-nothing committee," Oppenheimer testified in the hearing, after which he and DuBridge turned over to Rockefeller the written recommendations of the committee, including a proposal that the group be disbanded. "We thought we were dead," said Oppenheimer. "We were, but not quite." [7]

Meanwhile President Eisenhower radically altered the familiar role of the Joint Chiefs of Staff. Traditionally the Joint Chiefs had been appointed to fixed two-year terms; the appointments were staggered to avoid a turnover of all service chiefs at the same time; and the chiefs had been expected to provide advice to the President and Secretary of Defense on objective and exclusively military grounds without reference to political or other considerations.

President Eisenhower appointed a new set of Chiefs of Staff to serve indefinite terms at his pleasure, and he let it be known, circumspectly but unmistakably, through his Secretary of Defense, that the Joint Chiefs of Staff henceforth would be looked upon as members of the administration's new team.

As chairman of the Joint Chiefs, President Eisenhower chose Admiral Radford who, despite his earlier role in the Admiral's Revolt, had become a Big-Bomb-and-short-war man. Under the new approach, according to General Taylor:

> . . . The Chairman has come to be a sort of party whip, charged with conveying the party line to the Chiefs . . . Admiral Radford was an able and ruthless partisan . . . I always had a grudging admiration for his singleness of purpose and his undeniable effectiveness in driving through the programs of the New Look.[8]

As for the basis of the party line, General Taylor would write, "Hence the determination of the United States strategy has become a more or less incidental by-product of the administrative process of the defense budget." [9] This seemed to be Secretary Humphrey's version of how to arrive at a military posture.

As Admiral Radford was settling in as chairman of the Joint Chiefs of Staff, another key member of the new team was appointed chairman of the Atomic Energy Commission: Admiral Lewis Strauss. By the time Admiral Strauss took over in mid-1953, the National Security Council had approved the New Look and Secretary of State Dulles publicly had labeled it Massive Retaliation. It was the start, as General Taylor would say, of a "period of Babylonian captivity" for the United States Army — when "any collision of patrols over, say, Berlin would automatically result in general atomic war" — and when dissenting views within the Joint Chiefs would be dealt with in a style "worthy of the best traditions of Tammany Hall." [10]

Before the Eisenhower administration was over, two Army chiefs of staff, General Ridgway and his successor, General Taylor, would resign to carry their protests to the public. In effect they separately would say that the United States should be prepared to fight more than one kind of war, the United States should have some flexibility in its response to an outbreak of violence, nuclear and conventional forces must be balanced to avoid a choice between nuclear war or nothing, the United States should look to defensive as well as offensive weapons, the dogma of Massive Retaliation makes no sense from a military viewpoint and is merely the product of air power doctrine sanctified by a passion for economy.

Curiously enough, Oppenheimer had four-star allies throughout his struggle for the kind of national defense policy he originally advocated in his letter to the General Board of the Navy in 1948. A few, like Admiral Oftsie, tried to speak out early in the game during the Admiral's Revolt. Others, like Generals Ridgway and Taylor, would carry on the hidden struggle within the classified confines of the Joint Chiefs of Staff; and ultimately they would speak out too.

But not in 1953.

14

The Great Weapons Heresy

In the late afternoon of February 17, 1953, J. Robert Oppenheimer codified and reinforced his major offenses against the prevailing national security policy of the day. Without revealing classified information, he laid before an audience the issues as he saw them. He then added a stunning heretical prophesy about the future course of the nuclear arms race. It turned out to be the climax of an epic personal struggle to comprehend the impact of science upon tradition in the atomic age, and to open up the subject for public discussion.

There was none of the excitement of those days of discovery at Göttingen.

There was little of the tension of the last hours leading up to the great blast at Alamogordo.

There was nothing like the torment of Oppenheimer's struggle to contain his own handiwork during the labors of the Acheson-Lilienthal panel — nor the deliberate drama of the opening day of the UN Atomic Energy Commis-

sion when the Baruch Plan was presented as a choice between the quick and the dead.

The setting of Oppenheimer's excursion into heresy was a
weekly meeting of the Council on Foreign Relations in
New York. In 1953, the Council on Foreign Relations had
existed for well over a quarter of a century and had become
something of a national institution. Most of its membership
would be recognized by an average serious reader of
the newspapers; the rest are known to students of world affairs. Members come mainly from business, banking, edu-
cational, and professional life. A few are senior members of
the United States Foreign Service, and many more have interrupted private life once or more to serve in important
government positions. The membership in 1953, for example, included John Foster Dulles, Allan Dulles, and Admiral
Strauss. Every Secretary of State since the First World War
has met with the council, and it has few meetings not attended by members serving in high posts in Washington.

Indeed, the affairs of the council are sometimes difficult
to distinguish from the affairs of state. In the early days of
the Second World War, when the Department of State
had no research, analysis, or policy planning resources, the
council undertook a series of privately financed postwar
studies on behalf of the government.

So it was something of an understatement when John W.
Davis, long a director, wrote in his foreword to a short history of the first twenty-five years of the council: ". . . the
ideas exchanged and the conclusions reached inevitably
find their way into the nation's pool of useful knowledge."
In fact, at the time in question, the Council on Foreign
Relations had just established a panel which, in the words

of its chairman, John J. McCloy, "would quietly study this whole problem of our relations with the Soviet, to see if we could do anything that would be of benefit to the government or to general public opinion in that field." The panel included representatives of the State Department and the armed services, corporation executives, college presidents and professors, and such notables as W. Averell Harriman, wartime ambassador to Moscow. It also included Robert Oppenheimer, asked to join because of his special knowledge of nuclear affairs. In the course of the hearings, McCloy would speak of Oppenheimer's participation in the work of the Soviet study panel:

> . . . he was very much concerned about the security position of the United States. He pressed vigorously for not letting down our guard . . . if there was to be any negotiation, be certain that we were armed and well prepared before we went to such a conference. Indeed I have the impression that he, with one or two others, was somewhat more, shall I say, militant than some of the other members of the group . . .[1]

On the occasion in question, Oppenheimer gave an off-the-record lecture on "Atomic Energy and American Foreign Policy"; the "presider" for the afternoon was a member of the council, David Lilienthal.

Oppenheimer's concern about the failure to bring atomic energy under international control was well known. Lilienthal had seen him as a "tragic figure" in the "great drama" of Soviet rejection of the Baruch Plan; then found him "frantic" at news of Soviet acquisition of the atomic bomb. Nothing had happened in the interim to soothe his concerns; on the contrary.

Oppenheimer suffered no illusions about early prospects

for agreement with the Soviet Union about nuclear energy
or anything else; he was more "militant" than most of his
colleagues on the Soviet Study Panel; he accepted the need
for an extremely powerful nuclear strike force; and he conceded the necessity for tight secrecy over military aspects
of atomic energy as long as world affairs were trapped in
the assumption that great power interests necessarily are in
conflict. For all his disagreement with the doctrine of Massive Retaliation, he could see no available alternative to a
nuclear arms race.

From his deep knowledge of atomic science and nuclear
weaponry, however, Oppenheimer could see something that
not many others could see. Most of what he talked about at
the Council on Foreign Relations may seem obvious a decade and a half later, but in early 1953 his was a vision of
traumatic proportions.

The predictable fact was that if nothing happened to de-
flect the two super powers from the course on which they
were then set, the stakes would be no less than the fate of
whole societies and quite probably the accumulated civilization of the Northern Hemisphere. Two nations were on
their way toward acquiring a capacity for mutual destruction and a war between them would be mutual suicide. The
whole concept of victory would enter the realm of mythology;
the traditional purpose of war would become an illusion.

The foreseeable predicament to which the arms race was
leading would raise prospects even more difficult to grasp.

Once the United States and the Soviet Union had the power
to destroy each other — and thus accomplish their maximum
conceivable military missions — what would it mean to
"stay ahead"? Of what?

Would the arms race continue until each had a capacity to "overkill" the enemy — to destroy him twice, three times, seven times over?

And that isn't all. Even the surrealist vision of "overkill," if one could grasp it, rested upon calculations, however complex, expressed in quantitative terms; and the situation which Oppenheimer foresaw in 1953 raised wholly new questions of a qualitative and conceptional character — radical and perplexing questions that went to the roots of military and political tradition, to the very meaning of terms like "balance of power" and "strategic interests."

How could either of two nations with the power to destroy each other, regardless of who struck first, ever achieve a "favorable balance of power" in relation to the other?

What difference would it make anymore if one side had five, ten, or a hundred times more power than the other, if the "inferior" side already had the usable power to effectively destroy the "superior" side as well?

At this point, the traditional foundation for national security came into question; the whole motivation of the arms race seemed to disappear; the classical method of quantitative calculation of military strength seemed irrelevant — at least as far as strategic nuclear weapons were concerned.

The shocking prospect was that somewhere down the road on which the major powers were traveling was a point at which they would reach a qualitative kind of parity at the level of near-absolute power, a point where the search for superiority would meet a blank wall, where further additions to nuclear stockpiles would add nothing to national security, where numbers would no longer have meaning. Armament beyond what was needed to destroy an enemy who struck first surely would be, as Lilienthal thought about the H-bomb, mere "technological gadgetry." Beyond that point was a doctrinal void.

One might well have said of that predictable state of affairs in the field of security policy what Pascal Jourdan had said of the field of physics during the Golden Age at Göttingen: "wholly new processes of thought, beyond all the previous notions . . . would be needed."

By early 1953, Oppenheimer had become all but obsessed by the need to discuss publicly the revolutionary impact of the nuclear age upon the whole field of international relations. He was close to total frustration, and his every instinct impelled him to speak out. He had urged unsuccessfully a policy of candor upon the Executive Branch; he believed Congress should face up to the implications of what was in store; he had a touching faith in the value of public debate in the open society; and he could not quite bring himself to conclude that the rational method of scientific inquiry held no hopes at all for the solution of great political problems.

In the course of the hearings, George Kennan described his conversations with Oppenheimer about the pending decision on the H-bomb. Under reexamination he was asked if it were possible that Oppenheimer might have been "dissembling." Kennan said there was "no possibility" of this and then explained why:

> The reason I feel it is out of the question . . . is that I believed him to have an intellect of such a nature that it would be impossible for him to speak dishonestly about any subject to which he had given his deliberate and careful and professional attention.

. . . I have the greatest respect for Dr. Oppenheimer's mind. I think it is one of the great minds of this generation of Americans. A mind like that is not without its implications . . . for a man's general personality. I think it would be actually the one thing probably in life that Dr. Oppenheimer could never do, that is to speak dishonestly about a subject which had really engaged the responsible attention of his intellect . . . he is a man who when he turns his mind to something in an orderly and responsible way, examines it with the most extraordinary scrupulousness and fastidiousness of intellectual process.

I suppose you might just as well have asked Leonardo da Vinci to distort an anatomical drawing as that you should ask Robert Oppenheimer to speak responsibly to the sort of questions we were talking about, and speak dishonestly.[2]

The text of Oppenheimer's lecture is not available because the Council on Foreign Relations takes seriously the off-the-record rule which governs its proceedings. But *Foreign Affairs Quarterly* for mid-1953 published a version of it, more obscure and circumspect in content, less personal and emotional in style, than the lecture delivered to the council. In the course of the hearings, Oppenheimer said that he submitted the article to the White House for approval before publication and that no objection had been made.

Oppenheimer told the council that the United States was "in all probability, in a very tough fix." [3] He began by harking back to the time when "in the bright light of the first atomic explosion," men had the impression "that this might mark, not merely the end of a great and terrible war, but the end of such wars for mankind." Then he quoted Secretary Stimson: "Lasting peace and freedom cannot be achieved until the world finds a way toward the necessary government of the whole." He recalled that the United States had tried to consign nuclear energy to a limited government of the

whole under the Baruch proposals, but added that "these
have been very dead a long, long time" because "openness, friendliness, and cooperation did not seem to be what
the Soviet Union most prized on this earth."

Oppenheimer foresaw no early prospect of reviving proposals for nuclear cooperation because of the "peculiar obstacles presented by the programmatic hostility and institu-
tionalized secretiveness of Communist countries." Behind
these special obstacles were the "normal and familiar difficulties of devising instruments for the regulation of armaments in a world without prospect of political settlement."
Therefore, the idea of returning to the search for agreement
with the Soviets to control nuclear energy struck him as "irrelevant and grotesque"; and an "acceptable, hopeful, hon-
orable and humane agreement" to regulate armaments
seemed out of the picture.

Nor did Oppenheimer see any likelihood in the near future of "a happily prompt reform or collapse of the enemy."
The prospect was that "we are probably faced with a long
period of cold war in which conflict, tension, and armaments
are to be with us." And meanwhile, the nuclear arms race
was "in train."

Before "a reasonable amelioration or even alteration of
the great political troubles of our time," he said, a state of
affairs can be anticipated "in which two Great Powers will
each be in a position to put an end to the civilization and
life of the other, though not without risking its own." This,
said Oppenheimer, stemmed from "the character of the nuclear arms race" seen within the "time-scale of atomic developments here and abroad" compared with the "probable
time-scale of deep political change in the world."

This was the first part of his message and an old worry

with him: political change was not in step with technological change.

Oppenheimer had other things to say, things that he had said on other occasions in one way or another but which he would now state more directly and more critically than ever before. He would call not for mutations or adjustments in military policy but for outright "reforms."

For one thing, Oppenheimer had spoken often, in public and private, for at least a modest program of defensive weapons against nuclear-armed bomber attacks on the North American continent, not just to limit the damage and the casualties in event of an attack, but to help persuade the Russians in the first place that an attack would be too costly. At the Council on Foreign Relations, he singled out a high officer of the Air Defense Command and berated him for a recent statement to the effect that "it was our policy to attempt to protect our striking force, but not really our policy to attempt to protect this country, for this is so big a job that it would interfere with our retaliatory capabilities." This, said Oppenheimer, was one of the "follies" of the existing situation, the kind of folly that can only occur "when even the men who know the facts can find no one to talk to about them, when facts are too secret for discussion, and thus for thought."

He also had talked before of the virtues of openness and the dangers of secrecy in general. At the Council on Foreign Relations he struck out, in terms that he had not used before, against the whole policy of secrecy about the nuclear facts of life. He dropped the generalities and went to the point: "the inherent resources of a country like ours and a government like ours . . . are not available to-day" because of official secrecy about the nuclear arms race. As long as we live in a dangerous world, Oppenheimer said, some nuclear secrets should remain under lock and key. But he went on:

> . . . knowledge of the characteristics and probable effects of our atomic weapons, of — in rough terms — the numbers available, and the changes that are likely to occur within the next years, this is not among the things to be kept secret. Nor is our general estimate of where the enemy stands.

To make such information available, Oppenheimer said: ". . . we need the courage and the wisdom to make public at least what, in all reason, the enemy must know: to describe in rough but authoritative and quantitative terms what the atomic race is."

The first of the "reforms" which seemed to him to be "so obvious, so important, so sure to be salutary . . ." was candor:

> . . . candor on the part of the officials of the United States government to the officials, the representatives, the people of their country. We do not operate well when the important facts, the essential conditions, which limit and determine our choice are unknown. We do not operate well when they are known, in secrecy and fear, only to a few men . . .
>
> The political vitality of our country largely derives from two sources. One is the interplay, the conflict of opinion and debate, in many diverse and complex agencies, legislative and executive, which contribute to the making of policy. The other is a public opinion which is based on confidence that it knows the truth.
>
> To-day public opinion cannot exist in this field . . . I do not think a country like ours can in any real sense survive if we are afraid of our people.

Oppenheimer not only advocated openness about nuclear affairs in the United States but with allies as well:

> There is also need for candor in our dealings at least with our major allies . . . partly in order to explain to our allies that our atomic bomb will not do all things — that it has certain capabilities but is not the whole answer . . . This is surely a precondition for effective planning, and for the successful defense of Europe.
>
> Yet there are much more general reasons. We and our allies are in this long struggle together . . . and we cannot operate wisely if a large half of the problem we have in common is not discussed in common. This does not mean that we should tie our hands. It means that we should inform and consult. This could make a healthy and perhaps very great change in our relations with Europe.
>
> . . . It would be proper that the Japanese and the British and the many other governments immediately involved have a notion of what the issues really are.

What's more, ". . . It is also my view that it is good for the peace of the world if the enemy knows these basic facts — very good indeed, and very dangerous if he does not."

Oppenheimer proposed that the government tell the American public in "authoritative and quantitative terms" what the nuclear arms race was all about, "inform and consult" with its major allies about that "large half of the problem we have in common," and let the enemy know the "basic facts" about the U.S. atomic deterrent. In so doing, he was flying in the face of fiercely held tenets about nuclear secrecy.

For another thing, Oppenheimer warned for years of the dangers of placing too great an emphasis on nuclear weapons in overall strategy and forces of the military establishment. Now, at the Council on Foreign Relations Oppenheimer said:

Atomic weapons are not just one element of an arsenal we hope may deter the Soviet government, or just one of the means we think of for putting an end to a war, once started. It is, perhaps, almost the only military measure that anyone has in mind . . .

And this, said Oppenheimer, amounted to "a very great rigidity of policy" — barely a euphemism for dogma.

The big message was yet to come: and if the government would not talk, then he would. He would tell "what the atomic race is" and, what's more, he would do so without violating security. He knew a secret that could not be classified.

"I must tell about it," he said, "without communicating anything. I must reveal its nature without revealing anything and this I propose to do."

After alluding to what was public knowledge about atomic explosions in the Soviet Union and to official statements about Soviet production of fissionable materials as his sources, Oppenheimer said that it was his guess that "the USSR is about four years behind us" and its "scale of operations . . . may be something like half as big" as that of the United States.

"This," he said, "sounds comfortably reassuring. It sounds as though the job of keeping ahead were being satisfactorily accomplished.

"But in order to assay what it means, we have to know something of what it is they are four years behind, how fast the situation is likely to change, and what it means to be half as big as we are."

What it means, said Oppenheimer, was this:

. . . The very least we can say is that, looking ten years ahead, it is likely to be small comfort that the Soviet Union is four years behind us, and small comfort that they are only about half as big as we are. The very least we can conclude is that our twenty-thousandth bomb . . . will not in any deep strategic sense offset their two-thousandth.

This predicted the death of a historical doctrine that still taught men on both sides that national security lies in the attainment of military superiority over presumed enemies. It was heretical prophecy, and the traditional penalty for heresy is excommunication.

In his lecture to the Council on Foreign Relations, Oppenheimer ignored the advice once given by Frederick the Great: "When one speaks in public, he should consider the delicacy of superstitious ears; he should not shock anybody; he should wait until the time is sufficiently enlightened to let him think out loud."

Oppenheimer would not have welcomed that advice. He once told an audience that "in addition to understanding, man sometimes has a duty to act."

15

The Boom Comes Down

In retrospect, the best-known part of the Oppenheimer story is seen as anticlimax. For some seven years Oppenheimer had struggled to come to terms with the revolutionary force first let loose under his own driving direction; his failure was in the triumph of political and military tradition. His private positions on strategy and policy had earned him a host of impressive enemies. When finally he publicly prophesied that the day would come when twenty thousand nuclear bombs would not necessarily make a nation militarily superior to one with only two thousand nuclear bombs, the tale took on something of the quality of Greek tragedy.

There is a sense of inevitability about the fate of a prophet whose vision flew in the face of all historical experience, challenged official government doctrine, violated accepted guidelines for prudent national behavior in a hostile world, threw away the traditional criteria for measuring national power, and trampled on the face of common sense.

Yet Oppenheimer had proclaimed his view and threatened to go on saying it, which he did. During the course of the hearings, McCloy recalled Oppenheimer's position in the periodic meetings of the Soviet Study Panel of the Council on Foreign Relations in the spring and summer of 1953:

> The impression that I gathered from him was one of real concern that although we had a quantitative superiority, that that didn't mean a great deal . . . We were coming to the point where we might be . . . like two scorpions in a bottle, that each could destroy the other, even though one may have been somewhat larger than the other.[1]

Those who had the facts about the nuclear arms race might have been fallible and, in some cases, narrow and doctrinaire men. But they were men with the grim and purposeful assignment of staying ahead of the Soviet Union in nuclear armaments — men with their own convictions. From the military viewpoint, they believed that the security of the United States depended almost exclusively upon superiority in strategic strike capability with nuclear weapons. The best defense, they felt, would be a strong offense. The most critical and dangerous point in the nuclear arms race lay immediately ahead, and the strictest possible secrecy was essential to U.S. security. Any significant expansion of conventional forces or any major investment in air defense would be at the expense of strategic striking power, unless there was a huge increase in defense expenditures, and they either believed in a balanced budget or worked for men who did. Besides, this was official United States policy, approved by the National Security Council and endorsed by the commander in chief.

What counted for men who made this policy was that the United States had and must maintain a commanding lead in nuclear weapons over the Soviet Union. There was hardly time to worry about what the position might be a decade later. Speculation about a hypothetical paralysis of military doctrine at some future date, when the enemy was hell-bent on grabbing the lead for himself, seemed pointless and dangerous. Meanwhile, the less said about the whole thing, the better. As President Eisenhower reportedly felt about Operation Candor, there was nothing to be gained by public discussion of a situation which wound up at a dead end.

From a political viewpoint, the case for staying ahead seemed just as obvious. For those who knew and understood, it was not just a matter of a blind refusal of everyone but Oppenheimer to face the facts of life. The problem was not warmongering or brinksmanship or ignorance: the problem was to know what to do about the facts. Those who became the prosecutors of Robert Oppenheimer had a dilemma too, for the alternative to staying ahead was to accept a position of inferiority in the nuclear weapons field. Besides, it was the American arsenal of strategic weapons that made the NATO deterrent "credible" to the Russians.

How could a chosen course of inferiority in nuclear arms be conceived as a contribution to peace in a world in which it was accepted generally that competition was the name of the game of international relations?

Who could count on persuading the Soviet leaders that their own superiority in nuclear weapons would give them no ultimate advantage in the international struggle in which they believed — in which they had invested such great resources at such sacrifice?

Who was prepared to take on the assignment of explaining to the public, the Congress, the allies, that a decade or so later two thousand strategic nuclear weapons would count for as much as twenty thousand — that a nation could be as secure as an enemy ten times "stronger"?

What seemed to matter to nearly everybody was relative power measured by fantastic but still familiar numbers. And almost certainly this was the way the other side measured the "balance of power."

Oppenheimer looked ahead and foresaw the sterility and futility. He did not know what to do about it; but he wanted to discuss it out loud on the assumption that rational debate might somehow discover an exit from a blind alley — and history may never record a greater expression of faith in the open society.

Others looked ahead and could see nothing to do about it either, and thus no point in talking about it at all. The only thing that made sense was to be ahead and stay ahead, hoping against hope that the deterrent would, in fact, deter.

It is not necessary, or even instructive, to invade the arcane calculus of the "strategic nuclear balance" to understand the compelling historical, psychological, political, and semantic force of the traditional instinct to "stay ahead." And it was nothing less than this which Oppenheimer challenged.

Nor does it matter much exactly who the prime movers against Oppenheimer were, or just when a decision was made to move against him, or whether the event that triggered the case was faked or fortuitous.

What matters is that in the course of 1953, air power doctrine hardened into national defense dogma, and Oppenheimer challenged it; the nuclear arms race was headed for stalemate, and Oppenheimer predicted it; the very possibility of maintaining a meaningful superiority in strategic nuclear bombs would vanish at a foreseeable point, and Oppenheimer prophesied it; a small group of men, mostly scientists, knew the nuclear facts of life, and Oppenheimer was the most articulate, persuasive, and influential among them.

Powerful and purposeful men were looking for a way to still the voice of a critic, heretic, and prophet whose positions led at least some of them to question his motivations.

Oppenheimer's talk to the Council on Foreign Relations was toward the end of February; by May he was under direct public attack. Early that month the American Physical Society was holding its annual meeting at the Shoreham Hotel in Washington. During a break in the sessions, Rabi was crossing the lobby when he was accosted by Dr. Ralph Lapp, a nuclear physicist and member of the society, who had held several posts in the Defense Department. Lapp thrust into Rabi's hand an opened copy of the May issue of *Fortune* magazine which he had just picked up at the hotel newsstand.

"Look," he said, "they're out to get Oppie!"

The main title of the article was: "The Hidden Struggle for the H-Bomb." The subtitle read "The story of Dr. Oppenheimer's persistent campaign to reverse U.S. military strategy." The rest of it was what is known in the trade as a hatchet job.

To illustrate the first page of the article, *Fortune*'s editors found in their ample photograph files a picture of Oppenheimer apparently arriving at an airport at night. He was wearing a wide porkpie hat pulled rather low over his forehead. A heavy muffler was bunched about his neck and he carried a coat over one arm as though something might have been hidden under it. Oppenheimer's face seemed ghoulishly pale in the glare of the photographer's flashbulb and, because his wide-set eyes were diverted in a sidelong glance at the moment the picture was taken, wore a highly furtive expression. The net result was something of a caricature of a wily conspirator. On the following page was a photograph of an Air Force crew buckling on parachutes and preparing to board a heavy bomber. The caption read: "A SAC crew and their B-36 — focus of the American scientists' attack."

The article was unsigned. But in the course of the Oppenheimer hearings the author was identified as Charles Murphy, a member of the magazine's board of editors and its chief Pentagon correspondent, recently returned from a tour of duty with General Lauris Norstad of the Strategic Air Command. The text began:

> A life-and-death struggle over national military policy has developed between a highly influential group of American scientists and the military . . .
> The prime mover among the scientists is . . . Dr. J. Robert Oppenheimer.[2]

The *Fortune* article went on to explain that the prime mover was backed by a conspiratorial cabal with the code name of ZORC — four letters allegedly chalked on a blackboard by Dr. Zacharias in the course of a large meeting at which he was explaining the results of the Lincoln Summer Study. And ZORC, explained *Fortune,* was an acronym for Zacharias, Oppenheimer, Rabi, and Charles Lauritsen, though just why the code letter for Lauritsen was taken from his first name rather than his last was never explained.

In any case, when the time came for the Oppenheimer hearings, Griggs testified that he had seen Zacharias chalk the letters on a blackboard. All other witnesses present at the meeting testified that the first they ever heard of ZORC was in the pages of *Fortune,* and Zacharias could recall no occasion on which the four conspirators ever were together in the same room to discuss anything. (It was in this connection that Zacharias testified that he would question the veracity of Griggs.)

In other respects, the *Fortune* article was not without factual error; but it had its nuggets of inside information, especially about the H-bomb decision, the Vista Project, and the Lincoln Study. These events were used as background to bring out *Fortune*'s major charges against the ringleader of "the influential group of scientists" waging a "life-and-death struggle over national military policy." Said *Fortune*:

1. Oppenheimer tried to prevent the development of the H-bomb.
2. Oppenheimer wanted to divert nuclear resources from strategic to tactical atomic weapons.
3. Oppenheimer was in favor of developing continental air defenses, which struck the author as "a jet-propelled, electronically hedged Maginot line."
4. Oppenheimer was so swayed by moral considerations in his thinking about security policy that he favored a non-nuclear strategy and was even prepared, by inference, to sacrifice SAC.
5. Oppenheimer was thinking about things that a technical consultant should not be thinking about at all.

As *Fortune* put it in classical straw-man debating style:
". . . there was a serious question of the propriety of scientists trying to settle such grave national issues alone, inas-
much as they bear no responsibility for the successful exe-
cution of war plans."

Threaded throughout the piece was glimpse after glimpse
of Oppenheimer as the mastermind — a shadowy, slippery,
ubiquitous figure who, with what *Fortune* called his "disciples," was conducting a "persistent campaign to reverse U.S.
military strategy — that is, Massive Retaliation." Further,
Fortune stated:

Oppenheimer drew up the case against the H-bomb . . .

As the summer of 1951 wore on, the Air Force became conscious of a change in the atmosphere. The explanation was
soon forthcoming: the Vista group was conferring with Dr. Oppenheimer.

Oppenheimer had transformed Vista into an exercise for re-
writing U.S. strategy — an exercise introduced by a veiled suggestion that Air Force doctrine was based on the slaughter of
civilians.

Oppenheimer's thesis was that tactical atomic air forces, in
combination with relatively small ground forces, would by
themselves be sufficient to hold Western Europe against the Red
Army . . .

Vista's central proposition . . . had two unstated but obvious
corollaries. One was that SAC was no longer essential to material survival . . .

Sensing defeat in the Pentagon, Oppenheimer, DuBridge and
Lauritsen now sought the support of the man charged with the

defense of Western Europe . . . they turned up at NATO Headquarters with the Vista report . . .

Now came a shift in [ZORC's] tactics. Their object: to prove the feasibility of a near-perfect air defense for the U.S. . . . A nation that could be a fortress would not need an offensive atomic weapon.
It was . . . an extension in the U.S. of the Vista defense idea. The "fortress" idea appears to have germinated from the thinking of another disciple . . . [Dr. Berkner]

The essence of the ZORC idea is that the fortress concept offers a more moral solution . . . than does SAC.

. . . for the U.S., at this juncture in world history, to throw away its strongest weapon, merely because it is an offensive weapon, is a naive way to go about ridding the world of war . . .

The only individual heroes in *Fortune*'s story were Teller who, according to the article, "had perceived as early as 1945, at Los Alamos, the outlines of the theoretical solution to the fusion process," and Strauss "who in 1948 had displayed a sixth sense about the possibility of early Soviet success in this [thermonuclear] field."

The real hero of the article was the Strategic Air Command itself; as the writer summed it up with apparent relief: "And there the matter rests. Meanwhile the development of thermonuclear and fission weapons continues apace. And SAC, under General Le May, retains its mighty mission."

The boom was coming down — not on a teacher of theoretical physics who had hobnobbed with fellow travelers and contributed to Loyalist Spain, but on the Svengalian character painted on the pages of *Fortune*.

There was nothing in *Fortune*'s article about "loyalty" or "security" or "associations" or "character." It was, on the other hand, an extremely accurate forecast of the main lines of testimony by Griggs and the other principal witnesses called by the AEC against Oppenheimer in the "security" hearing that would take place nearly a year later. Lapp had gotten the point at once.

The *Fortune* piece appeared just before *Foreign Affairs* published Oppenheimer's prophecy made two months previously to the Council on Foreign Relations: "The very least we can conclude is that our twenty-thousandth bomb . . . will not in any deep strategic sense offset their two-thousandth."

Taken together, and seen in retrospect, the two articles dissolve the mystery of the Oppenheimer case. The government's action against Oppenheimer was too radical, too risky, and too uncharacteristic of democratic society to be motivated basically by a transitory political climate or by personal feud. A larger issue must have been present, and it was. The issue between the administration and Oppenheimer was on an epic scale: it stemmed from nothing less than the collision of the atomic age with military-political tradition.

16

"This I Cannot Do"

A GOVERNMENT AGENCY has an unchallenged right to select its own advisers. It also has an inherent right to change its consultants if — as was the case with the AEC after the adoption of the Massive Retaliation strategy — it does not like the advice it gets from its incumbents. Usually the problem is merely one of how to get rid of unwanted advisers gracefully and without embarrassment.

This would have presented no great difficulty for the AEC itself in the case of Oppenheimer. His only job with the commission after the autumn of 1952 was as a consultant on call at the initiative of the AEC. Such appointments are made under contracts with one-year terms. It would have been an easy matter simply to allow Oppenheimer's contract to lapse, using his services only occasionally or not at all in the interim. This point was clearly stated by Rabi in the course of the hearings.

". . . he is a consultant," he said, "and if you don't want to consult the guy, you don't consult him, period." [1]

But it was not that simple. Oppenheimer retained other

assignments in the fulfillment of which his views could be expounded and his influence felt; and his clearance for such work rested upon his access to AEC restricted data, that is, upon his "Q clearance." So whether the AEC consulted him or not, others could and would.

For one thing Oppenheimer was a member of the atomic energy committee which advised the special assistant to the Secretary of Defense for research and technology, a post then held by Dr. Whitman. When, in the spring of 1953, the White House issued Executive Order 10450, entitled "Security Requirements for Government Employment" and directed all federal agencies to review the cases of employees with "significant derogatory information" in their files, the security officials in the Pentagon dusted off the Oppenheimer dossier, which had become so fat that a summary of some fifty or sixty pages had been prepared by the FBI, and presented it to Whitman for review.

As Whitman told it in the course of the hearings, he waited until things were quiet in his office on a Saturday afternoon and then spent two hours or more studying the summary, "reading it very carefully and re-reading to feel that I had the significance of the file."

Whitman then wrote a longhand memorandum for Dr. Donald Quarles, who was about to succeed him in the Pentagon:

> Regarding Dr. J. Robert Oppenheimer. I have known for some time of the general nature and the salient features of the information contained in this file. It discloses nothing which would cause me to modify my previous confidence in his loyalty.
>
> Based on extensive associations with Dr. Oppenheimer over the past three years in the General Advisory Committee of the

AEC, and in the office of Defense Mobilization Science Advisory Committee, and in the Research and Development Board, I am convinced that he can be of great service as a consultant to the research and development work of the Department of Defense.

I unqualifiedly recommend his reappointment as consultant.[2]

Thus it appeared that Oppenheimer would go on being cleared under the new security order as well as the old —in the Eisenhower administration as well as the Truman and Roosevelt administrations — McCarthyism or no McCarthyism.

Apart from the Pentagon committee, Oppenheimer also still served on the Science Advisory Committee to the Office of Defense Mobilization which, instead of being abolished as the committee itself recommended, was reactivated in the spring of 1953 to provide guidance to the National Security Council. Far from being dead, as Oppenheimer had supposed, the committee was given assignments of a nature that must have greatly worried David Griggs. As Oppenheimer described those assignments in the hearings:

> The principal problems put before us were the proper use of scientific manpower, the very controversial and tough problem of continental defense, where there were several technical things that we were asked to look into and advise on and report on, and I think some other problems . . .[3]

Apparently the committee did indeed look into the "technical things" bearing on continental defense; for in the fall of 1953, the committee met with representatives of the National Security Council and, as Oppenheimer described it in the hearings: ". . . our principal job there was to make sure that the Council and its staff knew of technical advances which were useful in early warning and in radar generally and that they understood that some of the arguments against the feasibility of early warning were obsolete because of discoveries that had been made in the meantime." [4]

Oppenheimer still suffered from what Griggs and the *Fortune* article interpreted as a Maginot Line mentality. Meanwhile, of course, Oppenheimer was a member of the Soviet Study Panel of the Council of Foreign Affairs, where he tried to persuade his colleagues that the day was coming when quantitative superiority in nuclear weapons would not count for much in the military equation.

It was clear, therefore, that a decision by the AEC not to call on Oppenheimer for advice would not prevent others in the national defense policy-making community from seeking his counsel. Yet in point of fact the Personnel Security Board which eventually inquired into "the matter of J. Robert Oppenheimer" ostensibly looked into the possibility of a milder solution to his case. In its findings the board said:

> It seemed to us that an alternative recommendation would be possible, if we were allowed to exercise mature practical judgment . . .
>
> In good sense, it could be recommended that Dr. Oppenheimer simply not be used as a consultant . . .
>
> The Board would prefer to report a finding of this nature . . . To many this would seem the preferable line of action. We think that the answer of the Atomic Energy Commission to this question is pertinent . . .
>
> It seemed clear that other agencies of government were extending clearance to Dr. Oppenheimer on the strength of AEC clearance . . . it is said that were his clearance continued, his services would be available to, and probably would be used by, AEC contractors . . .[5]

One of the AEC commissioners, in upholding the decision to deny Oppenheimer access to classified data, largely based his conclusion on the point that he was a "top adviser to various agencies of government on national security policies." Commissioner Eugene Zuckert, in commenting upon the findings in the Oppenheimer case, discussed at some length the possibility of simply allowing Oppenheimer's consultancy with the AEC to lapse. But he wrote: "With his unique experience, his intellect, his breadth of interests and his articulateness, it was almost inevitable that he was consulted on a growing number of national security policy matters . . ." Zuckert found it "only reasonable to expect that he would be used in connection with broad assignments such as he has had in the past . . ." unless the AEC excommunicated him from the whole community of national security agencies by lifting his Q clearance.[6]

A simple solution to being quit of Oppenheimer's unwelcome and unwanted advice was not really available to the administration. Only a drastic solution would do.

Shortly after his meeting to impress the staff of the National Security Council on the new possibilities for beefing up continental air defense, Oppenheimer left for a lecture tour in Europe, primarily to deliver the annual Reith Lectures over the BBC. At this opportune moment a bizarre communication was received by J. Edgar Hoover. It was from William Luscom Borden — lawyer with a degree from Yale, bomber pilot with the Eighth Air Force during the war, former administrative assistant to Senator McMahon; for five years Staff Director of the Joint Congressional Committee on Atomic Energy; and the author of a book entitled *There Will Be No Time*. He was a student of geopolitical theory who believed that the only alternative to world government was world conflict in which strategic bombing would determine the outcome.

Borden had resigned in June of 1953 from the Joint Committee staff and was employed in the Atomic Power Division of the Westinghouse Electric Corporation. About five months later he composed his letter to Mr. Hoover. No one, with the possible exception of Haakon Chevalier, had quite such an exalted view of the vast powers of Robert Oppenheimer, of whom he wrote to Mr. Hoover:

> . . . In terms of his mastery of Government affairs, his close liaison with ranking officials, and his ability to influence high-level thinking, he surely stands in the first rank, not merely among scientists but among all those who have shaped postwar decisions in the military, atomic energy, intelligence and diplomatic fields. As chairman or as an official or unofficial member of more than 35 important government committees, panels, study groups and projects, he has oriented or dominated key policies involving every principal United States security department and agency except the FBI.[7]

Haakon Chevalier saw Oppenheimer in his postwar role as "the docile advocate of the Pentagon and the State Department" and described his government career as "an exemplary one of practically unswerving cooperation with a govenment unrelentingly committed to the eradication of communism." To Borden it appeared a bit differently, for in his letter to Hoover he said, "the following conclusions are justified":

1. Between 1929 and mid-1942, more probably than not, J. Robert Oppenheimer was a sufficiently hardened Communist that he either volunteered espionage information to

the Soviets or complied with a request for such information. (This includes the possibility that when he singled out the weapons aspect of atomic development as his personal specialty, he was acting under Soviet instructions.)

2. More probably than not, he has since been functioning as an espionage agent; and

3. More probably than not, he has since acted under a Soviet directive in influencing United States military, atomic energy, intelligence, and diplomatic policy.[8]

Borden did not play much of a role in the Oppenheimer case when it came to the actual hearing. In the classical style of the "mystery witness" in a murder trial he was, in fact, brought forward as the last witness for the prosecution. Neither Oppenheimer nor his attorneys had ever heard of the Borden letter, and counsel protested that if the Borden accusation were admissible as evidence, then the "hearing" should be transferred to the criminal courts; but the members of the Personnel Security Board had long since been provided with copies of the letter. The witness was allowed to identify himself and to read his letter to Hoover. This was the end of his role. No one seemed to have any interest in putting a question to Borden, and he slipped out of the Oppenheimer case as mysteriously as he had slipped into it.

Borden's letter had set in motion an irreversible process. Hoover sent the letter to the White House, Defense Department, and AEC. As Admiral Strauss, in his memoirs, tells about the next step:

In the chill of late afternoon on December 3, 1953, there was a telephone message from the White House. President Eisenhower wanted to see me immediately. Ushered into the large oval office . . . I found a meeting in session . . .

A bulky file of papers lay on the desk blotter. Indicating it, the President asked whether I was familiar with a report which J. Edgar Hoover . . . had prepared on the subject of Dr. J. Robert Oppenheimer.

I was . . . I had received a copy of the report directly from Mr. Hoover . . .

The report was a review of voluminous data concerning Dr. Oppenheimer, originally collected by the security staff of General Groves and then in the files of the Department of Justice . . .

Director Hoover's decision to review the record was the result of a sensational letter written to him on November 7, 1953, by William L. Borden . . .

The President indicated that he was very much disturbed by what he had read and asked whether the Atomic Energy Commission, as the responsible organization, had conducted a hearing on the charges as required by Executive Order 10450 . . .[9]

Executive Order 10450 did not require a "hearing"; an accompanying directive ordered all federal agencies to "review" the cases of employees with "significant derogatory information" in their files, the procedure which led Pentagon security officials to present the Oppenheimer file to Whitman for review.

In any event, according to Strauss's memoirs:

I replied that there had been no hearing since the order was promulgated but that the AEC was engaged in applying the directive to all employees. This, I added, would include contract consultants, such as Dr. Oppenheimer, in due course. The President ending the meeting, directed that a "blank wall" should be placed between Dr. Oppenheimer and any further access to Secret or Top Secret information until a hearing had been completed . . .[10]

There is nothing in Admiral Strauss's published account of the incident, nor in President Eisenhower's account in his own memoirs, to indicate that the chairman of the AEC mentioned that he personally had cleared Oppenheimer six years previously on the basis of essentially the same "voluminous data . . . originally collected by the Security Staff of General Groves"; nor that he had found this information irrelevant when making his recommendation of Oppenheimer for the post of director of the Institute for Advanced Study; nor that General Groves, Secretary Patterson, McCloy, and others had attested to Oppenheimer's loyal service; nor that he himself felt any embarrassment as the responsible head of a federal agency caught with a Soviet spy on the payroll.

When Oppenheimer returned to the United States from his lectures abroad he soon had an urgent request to see Admiral Strauss in Washington, and a date was arranged for December 21. When Oppenheimer called on the chairman of the AEC the only other person present was General Kenneth R. Nichols, a former deputy to General Groves in the Manhattan Project and then the general manager of the AEC. It was he who had sent the telegram ordering Oppenheimer's original employment on the Manhattan Project. Admiral Strauss tells the story of the meeting in his memoirs, documented by a memorandum for the files prepared immediately afterward by General Nichols and published subsequently by Admiral Strauss.

According to the Nichols memorandum of the conversation, Strauss told Oppenheimer that his case had been reviewed in response to the directive accompanying Executive Order 10450. There was an apparently vague reference

to a letter from "a former government official" but no reference to Borden's "conclusions."

Strauss then showed Oppenheimer an unsigned letter,
prepared for the signature of General Nichols and classified
"confidential," which presented a long list of allegations
and concluded:

> In view of your access to highly sensitive classified informa-
> tion, and in view of these allegations which, until disproved,
> raise questions as to your veracity, conduct and even your loy-
> alty, the Commission has no other recourse, in discharging its
> obligations to protect the common defense and security, but
> to suspend your clearance until the matter has been resolved.
> Accordingly, your employment on Atomic Energy Commission
> work and your eligibility for access to restricted data are hereby
> suspended, effective immediately, pending final determination
> of this matter.[11]

Some three-fourths of the Nichols letter was devoted to
"derogatory information" in Oppenheimer's file covering
his old associations with Communists and fellow travelers,
his memberships and contributions to party-front organizations, his subscription to *People's World,* and so on.
Twenty-two of the twenty-four specific allegations had to
do with "associations." Most items in the catalog began with:
"It is reported that . . ." And in large measure the allegations reported back to Oppenheimer what Oppenheimer had
himself reported to the FBI years before.

Most of the remainder of the Nichols letter described
the procedures by which Oppenheimer could appeal the decision of the general manager if he wished to do so. A single
paragraph of less than 300 words in the AEC letter contained
an allegation of a completely different character: ". . . It

was further reported that in 1949, and subsequently, you strongly opposed the development of the hydrogen bomb . . ."

There were two seemingly peripheral elaborations. One was that "the opposition to the hydrogen bomb, of which you are the most experienced, most powerful, and most effective member, has definitely slowed down its development." The other was: "It was further reported that you departed from your proper role as an advisor to the Commission by causing the distribution . . . to top personnel at Los Alamos of the . . . reports of the General Advisory Committee on the development of the hydrogen bomb . . ."

As things turned out General Nichols, who signed the letter of accusations, denied vigorously that Oppenheimer's views about the H-bomb could have had anything at all to do with the case; Oppenheimer's prestige and influence were never explicitly described as "derogatory"; and the distribution of documents cited as evidence of departure from the "proper role as an advisor" had not been caused by Oppenheimer but by the general manager of the AEC.

Nichols noted in his memorandum of the conversation that Oppenheimer, after reading the letter, "commented that there were many items that could be denied, some were incorrect, but that many were correct." [12] The question arose in the course of the discussion as to whether Oppenheimer would do better to resign than to submit to a security hearing.

Of this Strauss wrote in his memoirs: "I felt unable to advise him. A resignation might carry connotations a hearing might dispel . . . Resignation would have left all the charges on the record . . ." [13]

Indeed. And so, predictably, Oppenheimer on the following day wrote to Admiral Strauss:

> DEAR LEWIS: Yesterday, when you asked to see me, you told me for the first time that my clearance by the Atomic Energy Commission was about to be suspended. You put to me as a possibly desirable alternative that I request termination of my contract as a consultant to the Commission, and thereby avoid an explicit consideration of the charges on which the Commission's action would otherwise be based. I was told that if I did not do this within a day, I would receive a letter notifying me of the suspension of my clearance and of the charges against me, and I was shown a draft of that letter.
>
> I have thought most earnestly of the alternative suggested. Under the circumstances this course of action would mean that I accept and concur in the view that I am not fit to serve this government, that I have now served for some twelve years. This I cannot do . . .[14]

A long charade would now be played out for the sake of form.

17

The Case Against Oppenheimer:

I

TEMPO THREE, at the corner of Constitution Avenue and Sixteenth Street on the northern edge of the West Mall in Washington, was one of those wretched structures tacked together to make emergency office space during the Second World War. The story goes that President Roosevelt authorized the construction of these eyesores on condition that they be torn down within a year after the end of the war. Most of them have since been removed, but in 1954, nine years after the fighting had stopped, Tempo Three was among those still standing. It housed some of the overflow staff of the burgeoning Atomic Energy Commission — crude quarters for custodians of the most sophisticated triumph of modern science.

It was here, on the second floor of Tempo Three, in Room 2022, which normally was used for staff conferences, that a specially convened Personnel Security Board held a "hearing" from April 12 through May 6, 1954, "in the matter of J. Robert Oppenheimer." The whole affair was supposed to be "confidential," though anyone who knew Washing-

ton knew that it was only a question of time before it would
become public knowledge. The *New York Times* had the
story on the second day.

On the morning of April 12, Oppenheimer arrived at
Tempo Three by taxi, accompanied by Mrs. Oppenheimer
and Lloyd K. Garrison, a partner in the New York law firm
of Paul, Weiss, Rifkind, Wharton and Garrison. Mr. Garrison was serving without fee as Dr. Oppenheimer's attorney.

The "father of the A-bomb" was ten days short of
his fiftieth birthday. His hair, once black and bushy, was
now gray and crew-cut; but the sparse frame, thin face, and
deep-set eyes sustained the impression of sensitivity that he
had always borne.

For three weeks running, Oppenheimer would spend his
days sitting in Room 2022, on one of those nondescript tan
leather couches that abound in government offices, while the
Personnel Security Board, the attorneys, and the witnesses
talked, listened, and argued about his life and his work, his
deeds and ideas and duties and views, his personal qualities
and character. Five times he shifted from the couch to the
witness chair. His own testimony covers about two hundred
and thirty pages of the published manuscript, just over one-
fourth of the whole.

Before the "hearing" was over, forty-four witnesses were
heard, and the trial reporters recorded over 3000 pages of
courtroom transcript.

The great bulk of the 997 pages of published transcript
recorded testimony related to questions of "associations,"
"loyalty," "security," "veracity," and "character." The
"Chevalier affair" was labored and belabored, in direct testimony and cross-examination, and tape recordings, secretly

made by Colonel Lansdale when he interrogated Oppenheimer on the subject a decade earlier, were introduced.

The prosecuting attorney worked his way through long
lists of people who had been, or were suspected of having
been, members of the Communit party or who had mingled
in the affairs of the United Front in the 1930s. Did Oppenheimer know them or not? Did he or did he not know that
they were party members or fellow travelers? Did he or did
he not attend this meeting or that rally? Had he contributed to Loyalist Spain through a Communist fund-raiser?
Had he belonged to the Teachers' union — been on the
board of Consumers Union? Did he subscribe to *People's
World?* This and much, much more of the same.

This material overwhelmingly dominates the official
documentation in the Oppenheimer case. It has been sifted
and resifted ever since to support claims that the government
did or did not make its case against Oppenheimer as a security risk, that justice was done or denied. The massive transcript is peopled with names of the famous and a few of the
infamous; it is sprinkled with incidents that are fathomable
only subjectively; it is shot through with legal, philosophical,
moral, and merely mystical commentary on the nonjusticia-
ble issue of a man's loyalty to his society; and it is endlessly
fascinating for what it reveals and what it obscures.

In the course of more than three weeks of hearings, the
AEC called only one witness to testify about the relevance
of Oppenheimer's past associations to his continuing service in government. This was Colonel Boris Pash who, by
the time of the Oppenheimer hearing, had served for nearly
a dozen years in counterintelligence work for the Army. The
prosecution made much of the argument that the witness's

long experience endowed him with superior professional judgment in such matters.

Pash was one of those who refused originally to clear Oppenheimer for his first government post until General Groves ordered his employment. He believed in 1942 that Oppenheimer's past associations disqualified him from access to classified information, and he never changed his mind. Even after Oppenheimer had been hired, Pash had recommended his dismissal from Los Alamos. He later proposed the assignment of two "specially trained" counterintelligence agents as ostensible bodyguards for Oppenheimer, so they could keep him under still closer surveillance. Anyone who ever had consorted with left-wingers should never be trusted by the government; but apart from Borden's unexamined charges, Pash was the only witness of that mind.

General Groves, called as a witness for Oppenheimer, still disagreed with Pash. He still thought that old associations did not compromise Oppenheimer's status as a loyal citizen, and that Oppenheimer was no more of a security risk than any of the other scientists who had evaded the compartmentalization rule of the Manhattan District.

Colonel John Lansdale, Jr., who was the senior officer in charge of security for the Manhattan Project and who also was called as a witness for Oppenheimer, testified about his early concerns over Oppenheimer's associations. After many interviews and strenuous investigations, he had satisfied himself as to Oppenheimer's loyalty. He talked of Oppenheimer's discretion with classified material, and about his "extremely cooperative" relations with Army security officials.

Oppenheimer's witnesses, apart from Groves and Lans-

dale, included Drs. Bethe, Bush, Conant, Compton, Du-
Bridge, Fermi, Rabi, Von Neumann, Whitman, Zacharias
and a few other scientists; former AEC staff official General
McCormack and Commissioners Lilienthal, Dean, and Pike;
some corporate executives who had served with him on
governmental bodies; and several others, including Messrs.
McCloy and Kennan.

None of these witnesses was in a position to testify about
Oppenheimer's associations during United Front days in
California, nor were they asked to. Their experiences with
Oppenheimer covered a period when his main "associations" were with high military and civilian officials of government and with colleagues in such organizations as the National Academy of Sciences, the Board of Overseers of Harvard College, and the Committee on the Present Danger —
all of which he had served in one capacity or another.

What they could and did testify about was Oppenheimer's contributions to American science, to the war effort,
to the Baruch Plan, to the work of the General Advisory
Committee and other official bodies, to the growth of the
American nuclear arsenal and the development of more flexible weapons systems, and to the evolution of a partnership
between scientists and officialdom in the realm of national
security affairs. They testified, too, in terms that at times
verged on adulation, as to his capacity for leadership, his
loyalty, his discretion, and his hatred of all forms of totalitar-
ianism and oppression, explicitly in their Communist manifestation.

Some of the witnesses were worried about more than the
fate of one man. The hearings began ten days before the
curtain went up on the Army-McCarthy hearings in the Sen-

ate; they were worried about the climate of the times.

Colonel Lansdale, for example, after characterizing himself as a "hide-bound Republican," said under cross-examination: ". . . I am extremely disturbed by the current hysteria of the times of which this seems to be a manifestation."

A Cleveland trial attorney with a reserve commission in the Army, Lansdale then told how in his early days in counterintelligence work during the war he had fought against commissioning known Communists in the armed services. For this, he said, he was "vilified" and "reviewed and re-reviewed by boards because of my efforts to get Communists out of the Army . . ." Then he said:

> We are going through today the other extreme of the pendulum, which is in my judgment equally dangerous . . .
>
> . . . I think the fact that associations in 1940 are regarded with the same seriousness that similar associations would be regarded today is a manifestation of hysteria.[1]

McCloy, for his part, was worried about the workings of the security system as such. "I don't know just exactly what you mean by a security risk," he said, adding that, "I know that I am a security risk and I think every individual is a security risk."[2]

Then he spoke of the "enthusiasm and vigor and energy" that Oppenheimer had instilled into the work at Los Alamos and raised the danger of a "security risk in reverse." By this, McCloy meant that a security system too rigidly applied could destroy the security it was intended to serve. As he put it:

> . . . you can't be too conventional about it or you run into a security problem the other way. We are only secure if we have the best brains and the best reach of mind in this field.

If the impression is prevalent that scientists as a whole have to work under such great restrictions and perhaps great suspicion, in the United States, we may lose the next step in this field, which I think would be very dangerous for us.

The chairman of the Personnel Security Board was not much impressed by such tangential brooding. He interrupted McCloy at this point to say that he would "respectfully and in the most friendly spirit suggest that we not wander too far afield . . ." [3]

In any case, these and other witnesses felt that something more was at stake than the continued access of one man to classified information. The whole climate of opinion and the security system itself seemed to them to be at issue. These concerns sprang from an assumption that this was, in fact, a "security case" to which a more or less explicit security system, with written rules and regulations and criteria, was the relevant touchstone. This was indeed the way the Oppenheimer case was intended to look to the participants and the public as well.

To Dr. Vannevar Bush there was an issue that went much deeper. Bush argued that the Personnel Security Board should not have accepted the AEC charge that Oppenheimer opposed development of the hydrogen bomb in 1949 as derogatory information. He put it to the board straight:

I feel that this Board has made a mistake and that it is a serious one. I feel that the letter of General Nichols . . . this bill of particulars, is quite capable of being interpreted as placing a man on trial because he held opinions, which is quite contrary to the American system, which is a terrible thing . . . If this country ever gets to the point where we come that near to the Russian system, we are certainly not in any condition to attempt to lead the free world toward the benefits of democracy . . .

. . . I think this board or no board should ever sit on a question in this country of whether a man should serve his country or not because he expressed strong opinions. If you want to try that case, you can try me. I have expressed strong opinions many times, and I intend to do so . . .

. . . Excuse me, gentlemen, if I became stirred, but I am.[4]

Dr. Bush was getting closer to the bone.

18

The Case Against Oppenheimer: II

THE PRINCIPAL WITNESSES called by the AEC in the Oppenheimer case were two physicists — Drs. Teller and Alvarez; two chemists — Drs. Pitzer of the AEC and Latimer of the University of California; a former chief scientist to the Department of the Air Force — Mr. Griggs; and a major general of the Strategic Air Command — General Wilson.

These men were selected by the prosecution after extensive screening to support the administration's case against Oppenheimer. The hard substance of that case is more likely to be found in their testimony than anywhere else in the documentation.

None of the AEC witnesses had volunteered to testify, and most of them expressed regret at being involved in the unpleasant business at hand. General Wilson said he found it "a very painful experience" and was "exceedingly sorry that this is taking place and I don't think I would have volunteered to come up here to make statements of this sort." He said he "would like the record to show that I am appearing here by military orders, and not on my own volition." [1]

Pitzer said he was there "only at the very specific and urgent request of the General Manager" [of the AEC];[2] Teller said, "I would have preferred not to appear";[3] Alvarez said, "I certainly find it an unpleasant duty . . . I was asked by General Nichols to come";[4] and Griggs said he was appearing in response to a subpoena from the board.[5]

There are a number of remarkable things to be said about these witnesses as a group, given the fact that the case ostensibly was about the possible "security risk" inherent in Oppenheimer's left-wing associations, mainly in California in the 1930s.

For one thing, not one of them was qualified to testify about any of the first twenty-two of the twenty-four accusations made against Oppenheimer; and the matter of "associations" simply did not arise in the course of their testimony.

For another thing, all of them attested — voluntarily or in response to questions — to Oppenheimer's loyalty, and none doubted his discretion with classified information. As Wilson put it: "In fact, sir, it seems to me he has demonstrated his loyalty . . . in the tremendous job he has done for this country . . ."[6]

On the other hand, what was common to all was that they consistently had been on the opposite side from Oppenheimer in the long series of "hidden struggles" over military policy, strategy, and weapons development which preceded the adoption of the doctrine of Massive Retaliation. To a man, they were convinced that total war was the major contingency on which U.S. military strategy should be based.

The most remarkable thing of all is that each voluntarily disqualified himself as an objective witness on the very subjects about which the AEC had called him to testify. General Wilson laid it on the line.

He was, he said, a "dedicated airman" and "primarily a big bomb man." He believed, he said, in a concept of war derived from Douhet, Mitchell, and Mahan and he insisted that this must be understood "or my testimony doesn't make sense" because "it is against this thinking that I have to judge Dr. Oppenheimer's judgments."

To make it more than plain, Wilson said, ". . . I am not talking about loyalty. I want this clearly understood . . . this is a matter of my judgment versus Dr. Oppenheimer's judgment." [7]

When Griggs was called to the stand he said: "The testimoney I have to give here . . . will be concerned at least in part with two very controversial issues in which I was a participant . . . on the opposite side from Dr. Oppenheimer . . . I want to make it clear that I . . . may not be fully capable of objectivity." [8] A bit later he repeated the point: "I have already tried to give the Board the impression that I may not be a thoroughly objective witness in controversial matters, and this was a controversial matter . . ." [9] Again: "Let me make clear or let me emphasize that at this time I was on the opposite side of the controversy . . ." [10] And once more: "I am not without bias in this field . . ." [11]

Teller said that his thoughts about Oppenheimer's future were based on "feelings, emotions and prejudices"; [12] he said that he had "thoroughly disagreed" with Oppenheimer "in numerous issues"; [13] and he began his testimony about the role of the General Advisory Committee by commenting that "perhaps I am prejudiced in this matter." [14]

Alvarez stated that he had been in "serious disagreement" with Oppenheimer in the course of their work together, though he conceded this was precisely why Oppenheimer had sought his views.

Pitzer said at one point: "Personally, I would not rate Dr. Oppenheimer's importance in this field very high for the rather personal reason, I suspect, that I have disagreed with a good many of his important positions . . ."[15]

Nonetheless, the AEC's prosecuting attorney led the witnesses through their paces and drew out the sources of disagreement between them and Oppenheimer. Wilson was quite explicit about the cases in which their judgments clashed. For one thing, he said, "First was my awareness that Dr. Oppenheimer was interested in what I call the internationalizing of atomic energy, this at a time when the United States had a monopoly . . . This was a concern."[16] Wilson's next concern was over Oppenheimer's lack of enthusiasm for "two or three" of the range of devices that the Air Force wanted to develop to detect Soviet nuclear explosions.[17] He added the point that Oppenheimer was more favorably disposed toward nuclear-powered ships than nuclear-powered aircraft.

Finally, said Wilson, "The approach to thermonuclear weapons also caused some concern. Dr. Oppenheimer approached this . . . for technical reasons [with] more conservatism than the Air Force would have liked."[18]

In a touching burst of candor, Wilson confided that his disagreements with Oppenheimer were compounded by something else: "I would like to say that the fact that I admire Dr. Oppenheimer so much, the fact that he is such a brilliant man, the fact that he has such a command of the

English language, has such national prestige, and such power of persuasion, only made me nervous . . ." [19]

Teller's testimony turned mainly around the story of the Super. Going back to wartime days, Teller said, "Oppenheimer and I did not always agree at Los Alamos, and I think it is quite possible, probably, that this was my fault." [20] Yet from that time on, Teller seemed to feel that Oppenheimer somehow or other was impeding progress toward the thermonuclear age, though most of his evidence was based, he said, on impressions and hearsay; and he agreed that on occasion Oppenheimer had encouraged him to continue his work on the problem of the Super, had been helpful in recruiting staff, and had approved the push for a thermonuclear weapon once the theory made it look feasible.

Alvarez also testified about the H-bomb issue and deplored the lack of enthusiasm from Oppenheimer. He referred to a diary covering the period just before the decision to go thermonuclear and read out this notation: "Talked to Teller who . . . felt Oppie was lukewarm to our project and Conant was definitely opposed." [21] A bit further in the diary was this: "Particularly interesting talk with Oppie . . . Pretty foggy thinking." [22] In contrast to lukewarm and foggy views about the Super, Alvarez told of his participation on a panel chaired by Oppenheimer where he found "there was great enthusiasm for small scale weapons for tactical use." [23]

Pitzer also had much to say about enthusiasm as a qualification for consultants serving the government. He said he had "no personal knowledge of Dr. Oppenheimer going to Mr. X and saying don't work at Los Alamos" on the Super bomb, but it was "simply an inference" on his part that Op-

penheimer had not "enthusiastically urged men in the theoretical physics field to go to Los Alamos or other points
. . ." Because of Oppenheimer's prestige, Pitzer felt that
this failure must have somehow slowed down the project. As
he put it: ". . . I have difficulty believing that the program
would have had certain difficulties . . . if he had enthusiastically urged individuals to participate in the program, because . . . he was a great personal influence among theoretical physicists . . ." [24]

Latimer testified at length on Oppenheimer's "influence":
"You know, he is one of the most amazing men that the
country has ever produced in his ability to influence people.
It is just astounding the influence that he has upon a group.
It is an amazing thing . . ." [25]

Latimer said that Oppenheimer was "such an amazing
man" that he had "studied this influence that Oppenheimer
had over men. It was a tremendous thing." [26] This led Latimer to see Oppenheimer's influence behind "a whole series
of events . . . that started happening immediately after he
left Los Alamos." For one thing, said Latimer: ". . . Many
of our boys came back from it pacifists. I judged that was
due very largely to his influence, this tremendous influence
he had over those young men . . ." Under cross-examination, Latimer said that this point was "just an observation"
about "a matter I would not put too much weight on"; and
he agreed that the "pacifists" he had in mind were some
scientists who, after working on the A-bomb at Los Alamos,
concluded they had had enough of weaponeering.[27] But he
stuck to his views about Oppenheimer's mesmerizing powers:
". . . I have seen him sway audiences. It was just mar-
velous, the phraseology and the influence is just tremendous . . ." [28]

Speaking of the General Advisory Committee, Latimer said, ". . . Not only General Groves, but the other members of the committee . . . were under the influence of Dr. Oppenheimer, and that is some influence, I assure you." [29]

It was only on the basis of Oppenheimer's hypnotic influence that Latimer could explain the unanimous recommendation of the General Advisory Committee against all-out pursuit of the Super weapon: ". . . I was amazed at the decision that the committee was making, and I kept turning over in my mind how they could possibly come to these conclusions, and what was in Oppenheimer that gave him such tremendous power over these men." [30]

Latimer revealed a somewhat more personal contention. "One of the things that annoys a great many scientists more than anything else," he said, "is this statement that he alone could have built the A-bomb, or that he alone could have carried on the program . . . I am annoyed at that statement which has been appearing in the newspapers. Every time I pick up a newspaper and read that, I am definitely annoyed . . ." [31]

Though he volunteered the thought that Oppenheimer "is a very modest man," there seemed to be another gap between them. Asked why, at the time he was canvassing Washington offices in support of a crash program on the Super, he had not approached Oppenheimer and others on the General Advisory Committee with his views, Latimer said that he felt "I didn't have much influence" and added, "After all, a chemist does not have much influence with theoretical physicists." [32]

When his turn came in the witness chair, Griggs seemed to systematically follow the *Fortune* line. There was the story of the second laboratory, the Vista Report, the Lincoln Summer Study, the Air Force concern about "too much emphasis" on continental defense as evidence of a "Maginot Line mentality," the danger of outside consultants reporting to higher authority or "recommending budget allocations for major components of the Military Establishment," even a mention of "ZORC." And, as *Fortune* had done before him, Griggs complained that the scientists engaged in such projects as Vista and Lincoln were not "charged with the responsibility of considering in any detail or considering at all the fact of the activities of the Strategic Air Command." [33]

This was the burden of the case against Oppenheimer as it was presented by the witnesses selected by the administration, coached by the prosecution, and led through their direct testimony by special counsel for the AEC. It had nothing to do with the official indictment drawn up by the AEC but everything to do with the public indictment published by *Fortune*.

Much time has been spent in the wake of the Oppenheimer case in debating the legal niceties of the security clauses in the Atomic Energy Act, the criteria established by the AEC for clearing personnel for access to restricted data, and the then-new Executive Order 10450. There are enough ambiguities in these documents for argument. But the administration's case against Oppenheimer rested on a concept of "security risk" which had no basis in any law, regulation, order, criterion, guideline or interpretation legally extant then or now. Several of the AEC witnesses conceded as much in passing.

There was, of course, Wilson's flat assertion that "this is a matter of my judgment versus Dr. Oppenheimer's judgment," implying that personal security might be equated with conformity to views held by major generals in the Strategic Air Command.

Pitzer, in turn, backed into the new connection between judgment and security when he suggested in the course of his testimony that Oppenheimer should have resigned as chairman of the AEC at the time when President Truman ignored the committee's advice on the H-bomb. He went on to say that Oppenheimer's "position today would be better if he had insisted on at least some degree of disqualification in this field at that time." Asked by Oppenheimer's attorney to elaborate the point, Pitzer said:

> Let me put it this way. I am extremely sorry to see this issue concerning advice which on hindsight proved not too good brought up in connection with a security clearance procedure . . . This should have no relevance to security clearance procedure. If Dr. Oppenheimer had seen fit to insist upon stepping out of the position of advising on the hydrogen program, this could not be introduced into this argument at this time . . .[34]

Pitzer seemed to be saying that Oppenheimer should have quit in order to preempt the AEC from bringing him up on a security rap on grounds which "should have no relevance" to security clearance: "advice which on hindsight proved not too good."

The AEC prosecutor later put the following question to Pitzer: "You say very honestly that you personally disagree [with Oppenheimer]. Let me ask you whether or not events have proved that you were right or that Dr. Oppenheimer was right." [35]

Pitzer ducked that one; but the AEC attorney had somewhat better luck later: "Doctor, is it or is it not true in your opinion that in the case of a scientist as influential as Dr. Oppenheimer a failure to lend enthusiasm and vigorous support to a program might constitute hindrance to the program or opposition to the program?"

"There is a certain element of semantics in that question," replied Pitzer, "but I would say yes." [36]

Yet Oppenheimer had, in fact, resigned from the General Advisory Committee more than a year before being accused of giving the wrong advice; with or without enthusiastic support from Oppenheimer, the H-bomb had become a reality; and in the end the AEC reversed itself and insisted — despite all the time and testimony devoted to the H-bomb decision — that this matter, as Pitzer had stated, "should have no relevance to security clearance procedure."

It remained for Teller to illuminate for the record, even if dimly, the sense in which Oppenheimer was considered to be a security risk by the administration in 1953-54. Early in his testimony, under direct examination by the AEC's attorney, Teller gave his celebrated answer to the question: Do you or do you not believe that Dr. Oppenheimer is a security risk?

"In a great number of cases," Teller replied, "I have seen Dr. Oppenheimer act — I understood that Dr. Oppenheimer acted — in a way which for me was exceedingly hard to understand. I thoroughly disagreed with him in numerous issues and his actions frankly appeared to me confused and complicated. To this extent I feel that I would like to see the vital interests of this country in hands which I understand better, and therefore trust more.

"In this very limited sense I would like to express a feeling that I would feel personally more secure if public matters would rest in other hands." [37]

It was an answer that would convulse the scientific community for years to come. There was no question about what Teller was saying. At the end of his testimony the chairman of the Personnel Security Board fed the point back to him in question form.

"I believe," said Teller, ". . . that Dr. Oppenheimer's character is such that he would not knowingly and willingly do anything that is designed to endanger the safety of this country. To the extent, therefore, that your question is directed toward intent, I would say that I do not see any reason to deny clearance." Then he went on: "If it is a question of wisdom and judgment, as demonstrated by actions since 1945, then I would say one would be wiser not to grant clearance . . ." [38]

This was brand-new doctrine: *Security* clearance should be granted or withheld on the basis of *wisdom and judgment,* which could only mean, in practice, conformity with official policy. It would follow that any consultant, however loyal and discreet and regardless of services rendered, should be banned from the councils of government as a security risk if he disagreed with an official position.

Under that doctrine J. Robert Oppenheimer clearly was a major risk, for the administration knew very well Oppenheimer's thoughts about defense policy, military strategy, and where the nuclear arms race was heading. The administration also knew that Oppenheimer would not be silent and that he was persuasive and influential, which manifestly could only compound the risk.

19

The Findings Revisited

J. ROBERT OPPENHEIMER was excommunicated formally by a two-to-one decision of the Personnel Security Board; by a separate finding of the general manager of the Atomic Energy Commission; and by a four-to-one vote of the commissioners, whose majority findings were supplemented by separate explanatory statements by the three concurring commissioners.

The chairman of the Personnel Security Board was Dr. Gordon Gray, a lawyer-businessman, proprietor of several newspapers and radio stations, a former Secretary of the Army and, at the time, chancellor of the University of North Carolina. Gray ran the hearings in a generally competent and sometimes forceful manner, taking upon himself almost the whole burden of interrogation and comment on behalf of the board.

A second member was Thomas Morgan, retired chairman of the board of the Sperry Gyroscope Company. Morgan managed to listen to forty-odd witnesses for three and a half weeks without finding a single occasion for a substantive comment or question.

The third member was Dr. Ward V. Evans, a retired professor of chemistry at Loyola University, who did little questioning and most of that was either nostalgic in substance or directed at offsetting the impression made by General Groves that scientists as a group are a peculiar if not an abnormal breed of people. Dr. Evans dissented.

The report of the Personnel Security Board became known as the "Gray Report" and the chairman was its principal author.

The finding of the general manager of the AEC was, of course, signed by General Nichols.

The report of the majority of the commissioners is generally believed to have been written by Admiral Strauss. Additional thoughts and arguments were added by the two commissioners who signed the Strauss Report: Joseph Campbell and Eugene M. Zuckert. Commissioner Thomas E. Murray reached his conclusion by "my own reasoning which does not coincide with the majority of the Commission"; he wrote his own report. The fifth commissioner, Dr. Henry DeWolf Smyth, dissented.

The end result of the Gray Report, the findings of the general manager, and the statements of the majority of the commissioners is to leave the official case for the Administration versus Robert Oppenheimer in a state of doctrinal chaos.

The Gray Report is written in temperate language, breathing a self-conscious sense of heavy responsibility. It is organized under orderly headings, though it shifts back and forth divertingly from factual material to commentary bordering on the metaphysical; it covers the same subject in different ways in different parts of the report; it is not easy to match the final recommendations with the body of the text — and impossible to reconcile one set of findings with another. It is smooth, sometimes inscrutable, and hard to get hold of. With patient analysis, however, it disintegrates into a rag-bag of preachments and dicta, contradictions and non sequiturs, irrelevancies, and plain nonsense.

At the outset of its report, the board defined the general issue: "The hard requirements of security, and the assertion of freedoms, together thrust upon us a dilemma, not easily resolved." [1] The board observed that there are "two points of view" about the dilemma posed in the particular case at hand:

> . . . There are those who apprehend that our program for security at this point in history consists of an uneasy mixture of fear, prejudice, and arbitrary judgments. They feel that reason and fairness and justice have abdicated and their places have been taken by hysteria and repression . . .
>
> On the other hand, there is a strong belief that in recent times our government has been less than unyielding toward the problem of communism, and that loose and pliable attitudes regarding loyalty and security have prevailed to the danger of our society and its institutions. Thus, they feel that this proceeding represents the unrelinquishable opportunity for a demonstration against communism, almost regardless of the facts developed about the conduct and sympathies of Dr. Oppenheimer . . .

If the majority of the Gray Board did not consciously seize an unrelinquishable opportunity for a demonstration against Communism, it at least came down hard on the "security" horn of the dilemma. Indeed it asserted that "There can be

no tampering with the national security, which in times of
peril must be absolute, and without concessions for reasons of admiration, gratitude, reward, sympathy, or charity.
Any doubts whatsoever must be resolved in favor of the national security . . ."

What's more, the majority came to the rather breathtaking conclusion that its own deliberations had established the
principle that "the government can search its own soul and
the soul of an individual whose relationship to the government is in question with full protection of the rights and
interests of both." This was breaking new ground.

Not that the majority welcomed a state of affairs in which
the national security "must be absolute and without concessions." On the contrary:

> We share the hope that some day we may return to happier
> times when our free institutions are not threatened and a peace-
> ful and just world order is not such a compelling principal
> preoccupation. Then security will cease to be a central issue;
> man's conduct as a citizen will be measured only in the terms
> of the requirements of our national society; there will be no
> undue restraints upon freedom of mind and action; and loyalty
> and security as concepts will cease to have restrictive implica-
> tions.

The trouble was, as the Gray Report then put it: "This state
of affairs seems not to be a matter of early hope . . ."

Thus, for the nonce at least, the authors of the Gray Report resolved their broad dilemma by determining that the
goal of "absolute security" unhappily required "undue re-
straints upon freedom of mind and action." The Founding
Fathers must have spun in their graves.

As for the specific matter before the board, the Gray Report meticulously listed each of the items of derogatory information set forth in General Nichols's indictment and reported its conclusions.

With respect to "associations" in the 1930s, the Gray Report found that they were all true, substantially true, partly true, or probably true. Mainly it was a matter of the board's confirming what Oppenheimer long since had told the FBI about himself, his relatives, his friends, and his activities: yes, his former fiancée had once been a member of the Communist party; yes, his wife and brother and sister-in-law had been temporary members of the Communist party; yes, he had helped organize a teachers' union, and made contributions to Loyalist Spain, and been on the board of the West Coast branch of the Consumer's Union, and lent his name to United Front committees, and subscribed to or at least read *People's World*, and known certain people and attended certain functions and so forth. This covered all but two of the allegations against him.

After covering these points, together with the story of Oppenheimer's public service, the Gray Board concluded among other things:

1. That "Dr. Oppenheimer served his government because it sought him . . . The Nation owes these scientists, we believe, a great debt of gratitude for loyal and magnificent service. This is particularly true with respect to Dr. Oppenheimer."

2. That "the Board had before it eloquent and convincing testimony of Dr. Oppenheimer's deep devotion to his country in recent years and a multitude of evidence with respect to active service in all sorts of governmental undertakings

to which he was repeatedly called as a participant and as a consultant."

3. That "the conclusion of this Board is that Dr. Oppenheimer is a loyal citizen . . . The Board was impressed by the fact that even those who were critical of Dr. Oppenheimer's judgment and activities, or lack of activities, without exception, testified to their belief in his loyalty . . . we have come to a clear conclusion, which should be reassuring to the people of this country, that he is a loyal citizen . . ."

4. That "It must be said that Dr. Oppenheimer seems to have had a high degree of discretion reflecting an unusual ability to keep to himself vital secrets . . ."

5. That "We, as a Board, firmly believe" that "an individual who has been a member of the Communist Party, or closely enough associated with it to make the difference unimportant at a later time [can] so comport himself personally, so clearly have demonstrated a renunciation of interest and sympathy, so unequivocally have displayed a zeal for his country and its security as to overcome the necessary presumptions of a security risk." To relate this proposition specifically to Oppenheimer, the Board said that "we recognize that 1943 conduct cannot be judged wholly in the light of 1954 conditions . . ."

At another point, the Gray Report asserted, as though there were some constitutional question about it, another general proposition: ". . . The Board wishes strongly to record its profound and positive view that no man should be tried for the expression of his opinions." As the board noted elsewhere, this applied even to opinions about H-bombs: "We must make it clear that we do not question Dr. Oppenheimer's right to the opinions he held with respect to the development of this weapon. They were shared by other competent and devoted individuals, both in and out of government . . ."

Since that took care of every point raised by the AEC, unless the allegation of being "influential" is considered as derogatory information, one might have thought that these findings dispensed with the Oppenheimer case.

But in his dissenting opinion, Dr. Evans wrote,

> I do not . . . think it is necessary to go into any philosophical discussion to prove points not found in Mr. Nichols' letter . . .
>
> We don't have to go out of our way and invent something . . . it is not our function to rewrite any clearance rules . . . we don't have to dig deeply to find other ways that he might be a security risk outside of loyalty, character and association . . .

That is precisely what the other two members of the Gray Board did. Having come to the "clear conclusion" that Oppenheimer was "a loyal citizen," they posed the hypothetical question: Can an individual be loyal to the United States, and, nevertheless, be considered a security risk? The first part of the answer to their own question was:

> Because the security interest of this country may be endangered by involuntary act, as well as by positive conduct of a disloyal nature, personal weaknesses of an individual may constitute him a security risk. These would include inordinate use of alcohol or drugs, personal indiscretion, homosexuality, emotional instability, tendency to yield to pressures of others, unusual attachment to foreign systems. The presence of any of these items would support a finding of security risk, even though in every case accompanied by a deep love of country.

The statement was unexceptionable. Indeed it could have been drawn straight from the security regulations and criteria, though there was nothing in the AEC's "derogatory information" to suggest that any of these "personal weaknesses" were relevant to the case of Oppenheimer. The Gray Board did make a passing effort to suggest that Oppenheimer had displayed "a susceptibility to influence," but the point was neither documented nor pressed, perhaps because the board simultaneously was asserting that Oppenheimer himself was so influential that even his passive attitudes could sway the behavior of others.

Apparently the board's reference to "personal weaknesses" was merely a way to pursue what Evans presumably had in mind when he said "we don't have to go out of our way and invent something," for the Gray Report went on:

> There remains also an aspect of the security system which perhaps has had insufficient public attention. This is the protection and support of the entire system itself. It must include an understanding and an acceptance of security measures adopted . . . It must include an active cooperation with all agencies of government properly . . . concerned with the security of our country. It must involve a subordination of personal judgment as to the security status of an individual as against a professional judgment . . . It must entail a wholehearted commitment to the preservation of the security system and the avoidance of conduct tending to confuse or obstruct.

The AEC, of course, had not accused Oppenheimer of withholding "a wholehearted commitment to the preservation of the security system," or of failure to subordinate his personal judgment to the judgment of any and all professional security officers. There was nothing in the security regulations on which such charges could have been based.

Nonetheless, the majority proceeded, as Evans put it, to rewrite the "clearance rules." There was a question, the board said: ". . . of Dr. Oppenheimer's understanding, acceptance, and enthusiastic support of the security system. Beginning with the Chevalier incident, he has repeatedly exercised an arrogance of his own judgment . . ." The evidence, whether it had any bearing on the case or not, was marshalled laboriously in the Gray Report:

1. In 1946, in the course of an interview with the FBI, Oppenheimer had declined to discuss a meeting he had attended on the grounds that it was "irrelevant" to the subject at hand.

2. Later, in another interview with the FBI, he had declined to discuss two people alleged to have been Communists, because as Oppenheimer said at the time, they were "dead and unable to defend themselves."

3. Once, while walking back from the barbershop in Princeton, he had bumped into two professors with left-wing backgrounds who had been called to testify before the House Un-American Activities Committee and a brief conversation had ensued among them.

4. At another time he had written a letter to a newspaper to argue that a professor of physics at the University of Rochester should not be fired from the faculty because of previous political beliefs.

5. In 1953, Mr. and Mrs. Oppenheimer had lunch in Paris with their old friends the Chevaliers.

This, said the Gray Report, ". . . is not the kind of thing that our security system permits on the part of one who customarily has access to information of the highest classification," even one who had "a high degree of discretion reflecting an unusual ability to keep to himself vital secrets."

Not that the security regulations say anything about lunching with a friend who was a one-time fellow traveler, or about speaking to colleagues on a street corner; it was just the report's way of showing that Oppenheimer had failed to demonstrate "enthusiastic support of the security system" — something not required by any known law, order, regulation, or criterion for judging security cases.

The Gray Report was forwarded to the AEC on May 27, 1953. On June 12, the general manager sent to the AEC commissioners his own finding. General Nichols emphatically agreed with the Gray Board's "profound and positive view" that, in principle at least, "no man should be tried for the expression of his opinions."

"Technical opinions," Nichols wrote, "have no security implications unless they are reflections of sinister motives . . . I find that the evidence establishes no sinister motives on the part of Dr. Oppenheimer in his attitude on the hydrogen bomb, either before or after the President's decision . . ."

Clearly General Nichols was withdrawing, on each count, his own accusation that Oppenheimer "strongly opposed the development of the hydrogen bomb: (1) on moral grounds, (2) by claiming that it was not feasible, (3) by claiming that there were insufficient facilities and scientific personnel to carry on the development, and (4) that it was not politically desirable."

In any case, Nichols stuck with the ostensible case against

Oppenheimer: "He admits that he was a fellow-traveller and . . . The record indicates that Dr. Oppenheimer was a Communist in every respect except for the fact that he did not carry a party card." Yet in his final conclusion Nichols found a new way to formulate the urgent need for stringent security precautions.

". . . I have given consideration to the nature of the cold war in which we are engaged with communism and Communist Russia and the horrible prospects of hydrogen bomb warfare if all-out war should be forced upon us. From these things a need results to eliminate from classified work any individuals who might endanger the common defense or security . . ."

It was not a startling proposition, but its relevance to the case at hand was hard to perceive. Nichols said in his report that during the war Oppenheimer had been "of tremendous value and absolutely essential" to the U.S. Government; was he now saying that there was something in the "nature of the cold war" that required the same government to fire that man? General Groves had told the Gray Board that he had not considered Oppenheimer in the "calculated risk" category even in the early days of the war; was Nichols now saying that "the horrible prospects of hydrogen bomb warfare" somehow made Oppenheimer more of a risk than he had been in preatomic times?

Two weeks after Nichols forwarded his opaque final conclusion to the commission, three of the five commissioners concluded that "Dr. Oppenheimer is not entitled to the continued confidence of the Government and of this Commission because of the proof of fundamental defects in his character."

The main part of the majority report, to all intents and purposes, cited six items of "derogatory information," beginning with the "Chevalier incident" and including the letter to the newspaper in Rochester, in support of the contention that "Dr. Oppenheimer has consistently placed himself outside the rules which govern others," and by inference, in this way revealed his "fundamental defects" of character. The majority report then hinted that all the evidence was not produced at the hearing: "The catalog does not begin and end with these six examples," it said.

Dr. Smyth had a word to say about this in his dissent: "Any implication that these are illustrations only and that further substantial evidence exists in the investigative files to support these charges is unfounded." Smyth, of course, had access to the same documents as did the other commissioners; one could easily infer that he was questioning the veracity of the chairman of the AEC.

In any event, the majority of the commissioners flatly dismissed the very idea that Oppenheimer's opinion about the H-bomb had any bearing on the case at all, regardless of the Nichols letter. Admiral Strauss stuck with the straightforward position that a fellow who had consorted with Communists, and had told a cock-and-bull story to a security officer, and had not made a personal break with Haakon Chevalier, was not a fellow to be trusted in 1954 no matter how many times he had been cleared before, or by whom.

Commissioner Campbell, in his concurring opinion, had one point of substance which added a further touch of pluralism to the findings: "The finding, by the General Manager, that the services of Dr. Oppenheimer are not indispensable to the atomic energy program, is compelling," he wrote. But otherwise Commissioner Campbell's statement was devoted to explaining his own view of the proper role of the commission in security case procedures, which apparently was at variance with the understanding of his fellow commissioners. "The reponsibility of a Commissioner of the Atomic Energy Commission in a proceeding of this type is, in my view, an appellate responsibility." Finding no reason not to honor the findings of the Personnel Security Board or not to support the General Manager, Mr. Campbell joined the majority without further argument.

Commissioner Zuckert, on the other hand, had more of substance to say. He was preparing to leave the commission and he said: "It is a source of real sadness to me that my last act as a public official should be participation in the determination of this matter, involving as it does, an individual who has made a substantial contribution to the United States. This matter certainly reflects the difficult times in which we live."

Indeed, in the course of making "additional observations of my own," Zuckert found that security requirements were forcing "a change in our way of life." As he put it:

> . . . It is new and disquieting that security must concern us so much in times that have so many of the outward indications of peace. Security must indeed become a daily concern in our lives as far as we can see ahead.
>
> In this Nation, I believe we have really commenced to understand this only within the past ten years. It would be unrealistic to imagine that in that brief period of time we could have acquired a well-rounded understanding, much less an acceptance, of the implications of such a change in our way of life . . .

This would suggest that Zuckert considered it "unrealistic" to demand, as the Gray Board had, "an understanding and acceptance of security measures" and a "wholehearted commitment to the preservation of the security system." He apparently was not sold on the Gray Board's confident assertion that the "government can search its own soul and the soul of an individual . . . with full protection of the rights and interests of both," for he also said that "it will not prove easy to harmonize the requirements of security with such basic concepts as personal freedom." Nor did Zuckert find it easy to accept the Gray Board's flat requirement of "total security." As he wrote, "It will be a long and difficult process to construct a thoroughly articulated system that will be effective . . ." Besides, he said, "One inherent difficulty is that every human being is to some degree a security risk . . ."

Despite all these difficulties, Zuckert took the position, in effect, that where security is concerned, the whole may be greater than the sum of its parts. None of the charges, or categories of charges, against Oppenheimer would have led Zuckert to concur in the majority finding; but, he wrote, "when I see such a combination of seriously disturbing actions and events as are present in this case, then I believe the risk to security passes acceptable bounds."

Commissioner Murray had a radically different view of the whole affair because he had a radically different view of the meaning of loyalty. As far as he was concerned, he was the only man who understood what the Oppenheimer case was all about. Murray began his explanation-of-vote against Oppenheimer by taking his colleagues smartly to task:

> In my opinion the Personnel Security Board report and the recommendations of the General Manager as well as the ma-

jority opinion [of the Commissioners] do not correctly interpret the evidence in the case. They do not make sharply enough certain necessary distinctions. They do not do justice to certain important principles. What is more important they do not meet squarely the primary issue which the case raises.

Murray proceeded to argue with impressive eloquence that Oppenheimer's opinions in the H-bomb matter should not be held against him even if they had adversely affected the security interests of the United States. This despite the fact that General Nichols and the commission majority had insisted that these opinions were not, in fact, held against Oppenheimer. In any event, Murray wrote, in his own opinion:

> . . . it would be unwise, unjust, and dangerous to admit, as a principle, that errors of judgment, especially in complicated situations, can furnish valid grounds for later indictments of a man's loyalty, character, or status as a security risk . . .
> . . . in deciding matters of national policy, it is imperative that the views of experts be carefully weighed and never barred from discussion or treated lightly . . . even though Dr. Oppenheimer is not an expert in morality, he was quite right in advancing moral reasons for his attitude to the hydrogen bomb program. The scientist is a man before he is a technician. Like every man, he ought to be alert to the moral issues that arise in the course of his work. This alertness is part of his general human and civic responsibilities, which go beyond his responsibilities as a scientist. When he has moral doubts, he has a right to voice them. Furthermore, it must be firmly maintained, as a principle both of justice and/or religious freedom, that opposition to governmental policies, based on sincerely held moral opinions, need not make a man a security risk.

As for the question of "enthusiasm," in Murray's view:

. . . Government may command a citizen's service in the national interest. But Government cannot command a citizen's enthusiasm for any particular program or policy projected in the national interests. The citizen remains free to be enthusiastic or not at the impulse of his own inner convictions. These convictions remain always immune from governmental judgment or control. Lack of enthusiasm is not a justiciable matter . . .

The citizen's duty remains always that of reasonable service, just as the citizen's right remains always that of free opinion. There is no requirement, inherent in the right of civic duty, that would oblige a man to show enthusiasm for particular governmental policies, or to use his influence in their favor, against his own convictions . . .

Murray was clear about the imperfections of the security system as such. The system, he said, "is not perfect in its structure or its mode of operation."

Moreover:

Perfection would be impossible. We are still relatively unskilled in the methods whereby we may effectively block the conspiratorial efforts of the Communist enemy without damage to our own principles. Moreover, the operation of the system is in the hands of fallible men. It is therefore right and necessary that the system should be under constant scrutiny. Those who are affected by the system have a particular right to criticize it . . .

. . . the security system itself is only a structure of law, not a set of truths. Therefore this system of law is not, and must not be allowed to become, a form of thought control . . . No law or Executive order inhibits the freedom of the mind to search for the truth in all the great issues that today confront the political and moral intelligence of America. In particular, no security regulations set any limits to the free-ranging scientific intelligence . . . in its search for the truths of nature and for the techniques of power over nature. If they were to do so, the result would be disastrous; for the freedom of science is more than ever essential to the freedom of the American people.

So far, the passage might have been extracted from a speech by Robert Oppenheimer. Commissioner Murray then came to the "primary issue," which he said had been over-looked by the Gray Board, by General Nichols, and by the majority of his colleagues on the commission. That issue, he said, was loyalty; and he proceeded briskly to "define this concept concretely within the conditions created by the pres-ent crisis" — a crisis in which, Murray wrote, the "general definition of loyalty assumes a sharper meaning . . ."

The premise of the concrete, contemporary definition of loyalty is the fact of the Communist conspiracy . . .

The fact of the Communist conspiracy has put to the Ameri-can Government and the American people a special prob-lem . . . On the domestic front this problem has been met by the erection of a system of laws and Executive orders . . .

. . . those American citizens who have the privilege of par-ticipating in the operations of Government, especially in sensi-tive agencies, are necessarily subject to this special system of law. Consequently, their faithfulness to the lawful Govern-ment of the United States, that is to say their loyalty, must be judged by the standard of their obedience to security regula-tions. Dr. Oppenheimer was subject to the security system which applies to those engaged in the atomic energy program. The measure of his obedience to the requirements of this sys-tem is the decisive measure of his loyalty to his lawful Govern-ment.

No lesser test will settle the question of his loyalty.

. . . No violations can be countenanced. Moreover, the ne-cessity for exact fidelity to these regulations increases as an individual operates in more and more sensitive and secret areas of the program. Where responsibility is highest, fidelity should be most perfect.

. . . It [the security system] restricts the freedom of association of the governmental employee who is subject to it. It restricts his movements and activities . . . It restricts his freedom of personal and family life. It makes special demands on his character, moral virtue and spirit of sacrifice . . .

It will not do to plead that Dr. Oppenheimer revealed no secrets to the Communists and fellow-travelers with whom he chose to associate. What is incompatible with obedience to the laws of security is the associations themselves, however innocent in fact . . .

Dr. Oppenheimer occupied a position of paramount importance . . . It was reasonable to expect that he would be particularly scrupulous in his fidelity to security regulations. These regulations are the special test of the loyalty of the American citizen who serves his government in the sensitive area of the atomic energy program. Dr. Oppenheimer did not meet this decisive test. He was disloyal.

By Commissioner Murray's exegesis — and on General Groves's testimony — the scientists who worked at wartime Los Alamos were, to a man, disloyal; but then, as he said, he had arrived at his conclusion "by my own reasoning."

As might be expected, Dr. Smyth had a less apocalyptic view of the demands of the security system upon employees and those who judge them. And he quoted from the Atomic Energy Commission's security criteria to support it: "The facts of each case must be carefully weighed and determination made in the light of all information presented, whether favorable or unfavorable. The judgment of responsible persons as to the integrity of the individuals should be considered. The decision as to security clearance is an overall commonsense judgment . . ."

Smyth also knew what he meant by the term security risk. ". . . The only question being determined by the Atomic Energy Commission," he wrote,

> . . . is whether there is a possibility that Dr. Oppenheimer will intentionally or unintentionally reveal secret information to persons who should not have it. To me, this is what is meant within our security system by the term security risk. Character and association are important only insofar as they bear on the possibility that secret information will be improperly revealed.
>
> . . . there is no indication in the entire record that Dr. Oppenheimer has ever divulged any secret information. The past fifteen years of his life have been investigated and reinvestigated. For much of the last eleven years he has been under actual surveillance, his movements watched, his conversations noted, his mail and telephone calls checked. This professional review of his actions has been supplemented by enthusiastic amateur help from powerful personal enemies.

After boiling down the evidence, Smyth wrote that "I find nothing in the foregoing to substantiate the charge [by the Gray Board] that Dr. Oppenheimer has had a persistent and continuing association with subversive individuals. These are nothing more than occasional incidents in a complex life, and they were not sought by Dr. Oppenheimer."

While Murray found "exact fidelity" to the security system the only valid test of loyalty, Smyth wrote: ". . . I would suggest that the system itself is nothing to worship. It is a necessary means to an end. Its sole purpose, apart from the prevention of sabotage, is to protect secrets. If a man protects the secrets he has in his hands and his head, he has shown essential regard for the security system."

Cooperation with security officials, Smyth said, "is to be expected," but the security system has

. . . neither the responsibility nor the right to dictate every detail of a man's life. I frankly do not understand the charge made by the majority that Dr. Oppenheimer has shown a persistent and willful disregard for the obligations of security, and that therefore he should be declared a security risk. No gymnastics or rationalization allow me to accept this argument . . . Such a finding extends the concept of "security risk" beyond its legitimate justification and constitutes a dangerous precedent.

In these times, failure to employ a man of great talents may impair the strength and power of this country. Yet, I would accept this loss if I doubted the loyalty of Dr. Oppenheimer or his ability to hold his tongue. I have no such doubts.

I conclude that Dr. Oppenheimer's employment "will not endanger the common defense and security" and will be "clearly consistent with the interests of national security." I prefer the positive statement that Dr. Oppenheimer's further employment will continue to strengthen the United States.

The near-total confusion about the legal and extralegal meanings attributed to "loyalty" and "security risk," and the profusion of attitudes toward the "security system" which abound in the findings of the Gray Board, the general manager's report, and the opinions of the AEC commissioners have frustrated many who have tried to make sense of the Oppenheimer case.

With hindsight, however, one can find in the official documents traces of an infinitely more serious case against Oppenheimer than the catalog of left-wing associations in the 1930s drawn from his FBI dossier.

A hint of this is raised by Murray's long argument in support of a citizen's freedom of opinion and of moral judgment, of his right to disagree and even criticize the government for which he works, of his option to be unenthusiastic if he so chooses. Presumably Murray did not go into all this gratuitously.

In Commissioner Zuckert's finding there is another clue. What seemed to him decisive was not so much the question of Oppenheimer's past, but the question of his future. Zuckert, in his opinion, went carefully into the business of why it was "not practical" to dispose of the Oppenheimer case by allowing his consultant's contract to lapse. In so doing, he demolished the carefully labored allegation variously made by *Fortune*, the Nichols letter of allegations, and several AEC witnesses that Oppenheimer had "departed his proper role" as a technical consultant by dabbling in security policy and strategic questions. Oppenheimer, Zuckert made clear in substantiation of his point, was no ordinary technical consultant. Indeed, wrote Zuckert, Oppenheimer had a "unique place" both "in the scientific world and as a top government adviser . . . His advice was sought on many matters in which science or technical aspects of atomic energy were important, but important as incidentals and background . . . he was consulted on a growing number of national security policy matters . . .

". . . It is true that since 1953 the Commission has used him very little. Commission clearance has, however, been a basis for other agencies using him in connection with delicate problems of national security. It is logical to expect that would continue . . ."

This being the case, said Zuckert, it was imperative to pronounce upon Oppenheimer's future role in the community of national security agencies. As he said, "I think the Commission is clearly obligated to determine . . . whether scientists may continue to call upon him as they have in the past . . ."

The direct evidence in the official findings as to what the Oppenheimer case was about is found in the strange dichotomies of the Gray Report. On the one hand the Gray Report asserted:

1. That "no man should be tried for his opinions";
2. That Oppenheimer had a specific right to his opinions about the H-bomb and the Board did not question them;
3. That after the President's decision to go for the Super, "Dr. Oppenheimer did not oppose the project in a positive or open manner, nor did he decline to cooperate in the project"; and
4. That "the Board does not find that Dr. Oppenheimer urged other scientists not to work on the program."

In effect the board, after taking an enormous amount of testimony on a question for which it said no man should be tried, looked at the evidence and found that Oppenheimer was not only improperly charged but innocent to boot. Yet the Gray Report made this astonishing switch:

> We cannot dismiss the matter of Dr. Oppenheimer's relationship to the development of the hydrogen bomb simply with the finding that his conduct was not motivated by disloyalty, because it is our conclusion that, whatever the motivation, the security interests of the United States were affected.
>
> We believe that, had Dr. Oppenheimer given his enthusiastic support for the program, a concerted effort would have been initiated at an earlier date.
>
> Following the President's decision, he did not show the enthusiastic support for the program which might have been expected . . . of the chief atomic adviser to the Government under the circumstances. Indeed, a failure to communicate an abandonment of his earlier position undoubtedly had an effect upon other scientists . . .

As it happens, the board had before it sworn testimony from the director of Los Alamos, from the secretary of the General Advisory Committee, from the head of the military applications branch of the AEC, and from other witnesses to the effect that neither Oppenheimer nor the advisory committee had in any way delayed the development of the Super bomb.

Dr. Evans said flatly in his dissenting opinion: "He [Oppenheimer] did not hinder the development of the H-bomb and there is absolutely nothing in the testimony to show that he did."

In addition the board "Reluctantly concluded that Dr. Oppenheimer's candor left much to be desired in his discussion with the Board of his attitude and position in the entire chronology of the hydrogen-bomb problem." There was no specific explanation of this alleged lack of candor.

In the end, the purported lack of enthusiasm and candor appears to be no more than window-dressing; for when the authors of the majority Gray Report got around to listing the "considerations [which] have been controlling in leading to our conclusion," they fashioned an entirely new formulation for the H-bomb point: "We find his conduct in the hydrogen-bomb program sufficiently disturbing as to raise a doubt as to whether his future participation, if characterized by the same attitudes in a Government program relating to the national defense, would be clearly consistent with the best interests of security."

This was getting close to the heart of it. Here, said the Gray Report, was a controlling consideration in the action taken against Oppenheimer, and its authors could only be saying something like this: five years ago this man rendered a judgment which leads us to suspect that if he is allowed to remain in government service he might in the future reach other judgments which we would regard as not clearly in the interest of national security, and we therefore consider him a security risk.

Having righteously rejected the notion of trying a man for his known opinions, the majority of the Gray Board presumed to discern what his future opinions might be and condemn them in advance.

Of course the Gray Board did have something to go on when it came to extrapolating Oppenheimer's views on national security policy. Oppenheimer had counseled the government in 1949 and subsequently against overreliance on offensive strategic nuclear weapons and he might well be expected to do so again if he retained his position as consultant.

Despite all the elaborate verbal shrubbery of the Gray Report, its authors ultimately made their point in unmistakable terms. Discussing the role of a defense consultant in relation to government officials, they wrote: "In evaluating advice from a specialist which departs from the area of his specialty, Government officials charged with the military posture of our country must also be certain that underlying any advice is a genuine conviction that this country cannot in the interest of security have less than the strongest possible offensive capabilities in a time of national danger."

Obviously "the strongest possible offensive capabilities" meant Big Bombs and Massive Retaliation. It was stated again a bit farther on in the Gray Report: "We are concerned, however, that he [Oppenheimer] may have departed his role as scientific adviser to exercise highly persuasive in-

fluence in matters in which his convictions were not necessarily a reflection of technical judgment, and also not necessarily related to the protection of the strongest offensive military interests of the country."

When the contradictions and internal inconsistencies of the
Gray Report are peeled away, the central message comes
through: in 1954 the officials in charge of national defense
policy wanted no advice "not necessarily related to the protection of the strongest offensive military interests of the
country," i.e., Massive Retaliation, and all consultants must
begin with a "genuine conviction" that this is the one true
faith.

On June 29, 1954, the day before Oppenheimer's contract
as a consultant to the AEC was due to expire, the Commission announced that it had "reached a decision in the matter of J. Robert Oppenheimer." As far as the administration
was concerned, the case was closed.

20

Sublime Irony

THE OPPENHEIMER CASE is shot through with irony and paradox, with riddles and conundrums, and in retrospect it has its touches of drollery.

General Groves, for example, began his testimony in a case involving the security of state secrets by assuring the board that there was no danger of *his* saying anything indiscreet; and then proceeded to be indiscreet so often that his testimony had to be censored in seven places. In a case involving loyalty, he seemed to relish his volunteered account of how disloyal he had been to his wartime commander in chief by deliberately violating President Roosevelt's orders to keep the British fully informed of developments in the Manhattan Project.

Colonel Lansdale related how he had been guilty of "promptly violating" an order from General Groves "in a most un-military manner," in a case in which the accused was charged with exercising an "arrogance of judgment" about rules and regulations.

Drs. Teller, Alvarez, and Latimer made no bones at all

about having lobbied on Capitol Hill to build pressure on the President of the United States for a decision to go thermonuclear in a hearing in which the man in the dock was accused of having "departed from your proper role" as a technical consultant to the AEC.

Witness after witness swore that he had opposed the H-bomb for very much the same reasons Oppenheimer did, without challenge to his loyalty, discretion, or even judgment.

The AEC prosecuting attorney worked hard in the course of the hearing to build up the *bona fides* of Colonel Pash as a "professional" security officer, when it was the professional security officers who tailed Oppenheimer day and night but apparently never suspected Klaus Fuchs.

Obviously, if Oppenheimer could be fingered as a security risk in 1953, heads should have rolled in the FBI and the Pentagon's counterintelligence services for failure to provide evidence for such a conclusion after eleven years of unflagging search.

One is struck, too, by the bizarre position of Admiral Strauss who, in effect, confessed in 1954 that in 1947 he had cleared a security risk for one of the most sensitive posts in government and had placed a man with serious defects of character at the head of a major academic institution.

Surely it is one of history's bitter little jokes that Oppenheimer was accused publicly of trying to change military strategy when four-star Army generals were struggling in secret to alter that strategy in the same direction and would retire, with records and pensions intact, subsequently to reveal much more in public about hidden policy struggles than Oppenheimer even hinted at.

There is a certain bitterness, too, in the fact that by 1961 President Kennedy junked the policy of Massive Retaliation, recalled General Taylor to be chairman of the Joint Chiefs of Staff, adopted the Strategy of Flexible Response, restored a balance between conventional and nuclear arms and among the military services; and in the fact that a bit later, in the Johnson administration, the United States would start sharing nuclear secrets with its allies and NATO would adopt Flexible Response as preferred strategy for the defense of Europe. The bitterness may have been diluted somewhat for Oppenheimer when he was called for the second time to receive an award at the White House. In one of his first official acts after the assassination of President Kennedy, President Johnson awarded Oppenheimer the Fermi Prize for achievement in nuclear physics, the U.S. Government's most prestigious scientific award. This made a big story for the next issue of *Life* which concluded, in effect, that bygones should now be bygones.

If Robert Oppenheimer was, as they say in Communist societies, rehabilitated, the "Oppenheimer case" could not so easily be closed. The fundamental dilemmas of the nuclear age which led to his fall from grace would not go away. The heretical prophecy he made to the Council on Foreign Relations in 1953 would become a contemporary issue. Baruch's naked choice between the quick and the dead seemed unresolved.

It remained for Winston Churchill, with his uncanny instinct for political paradox, to put his finger on it all. In early 1955, speaking of the prospects for the thermonuclear age, he said, "It may be that we shall, by a process of sublime irony, have reached a stage in this story where safety will be the sturdy child of terror and survival the twin brother of annihilation." [1]

This was more than just another flight of Churchillian rhetoric; it was blazing insight into the political realities of life in the thermonuclear age.

Oppenheimer, dedicated apostle of the rational method, feared that nuclear weapons would lead to nuclear war before time permitted the forces of change to work their ways in the Communist world. Churchill, devoted student of history's wayward course, sensed that man's instinct for survival would carry the day. Oppenheimer prophesied a time of qualitative nuclear parity; Churchill foresaw that the political implication was a pax atomica. Sublime irony indeed!

For Oppenheimer, the ultimate irony was that he was accused of an affinity for a totalitarian political system when his only dogma was faith in the open society.

21

Between the Quick
and the Dead

WHEN THE UNITED STATES GOVERNMENT severed relations
with Oppenheimer, he could at last return to "physics and
the teaching of physics" which, he had told David Lilienthal, "is my life."

Oppenheimer had a number of offers to teach and live
abroad. He turned them down. Though he was excommunicated from government agencies and contractors, he rejected exile from the United States. "Damn it," he once said
to George Kennan, "I love this country."

Instead he turned his energies to the development of the
Institute for Advanced Study, and it has been said that in the
years following his dismissal from government Oppenheimer
built the institute into the world's greatest center of theoretical physics. No detail of the institute's affairs, including the
design and construction of new buildings, seemed to escape
his thought and attention.

During most of the period when Oppenheimer was exiled
from government, the nuclear arms race ran its insensate
course to, and beyond, the point of mutual capacity for mu-

tual destruction which he had foreseen in the early 1950s. With one side determined to stay ahead and the other to catch up, the internal dynamics of the arms race could only accelerate; action on one side induced automatic reaction on the other. Tests of "clean" and "dirty" bombs made their differential contributions to radioactive pollution. Guided missiles took over the leading delivery role from the airplane. "Hard" sites followed "soft" sites for underground missile silos and other nuclear warheads went underwater in Polaris and Polaris-type submarines. Poseidons, ABMs and FOBs entered the nuclear lexicon and the awesome calculus of the "strategic balance" was unknown to the public, impenetrable for the layman — and increasingly removed from political reality.

Sporadic efforts to bring the arms race under some measure of control came to nothing for nearly a decade. In 1958 the Soviets accepted a moratorium on weapons tests in the atmosphere, the kind of self-policing "simple agreement" that Dr. Bush had urged six years previously. Three years later, having used the time to absorb the lessons of their last test series and to prepare for another, the Soviets broke the moratorium on twenty-four-hour notice. In the ensuing two series of Russian tests, Khrushchev became the proud possessor of a ninety-megaton bomb, too big for even the biggest of targets. Reluctantly, President Kennedy decided he had no course but to follow suit; the United States resumed atmospheric testing too.

Intellectually, officials could grasp the meaning of the nuclear predicament prophesied by Oppenheimer; but when it came to political action, the old conventions prevailed. Toward the end of his tenure as Secretary of Defense, Robert McNamara explained with clinical clarity why additional strategic nuclear weapons could not add to the national security of either side — then vowed to maintain superiority over the Soviet stockpile of nuclear weapons.

Meanwhile, Oppenheimer's time scale for "deep political change" seemed to stretch ahead as far as one could see. "Standing firm" appeared to be the only safe way to confront a totalitarian state whose leaders paid first respect to military power and interpreted any probe toward accommodation as a sure sign of weakness. The "long period of cold war" postulated by Oppenheimer in the course of his lecture to the Council on Foreign Relations remained the prevailing condition. The outcome was stalemate, and for a time it looked as though the affairs of the Super Powers were in a permanent state of paralysis.

Yet the nuclear deterrent did, in fact, deter a terminal world war, and a *pax atomica* became, in practice, the sublime irony of the thermonuclear age. Provocations, incidents, and crises that almost surely would have led to war in preatomic times were handled with cool restraint in Washington and Moscow. Security, it seemed, was indeed the "sturdy child of terror."

In retrospect, then, it can be argued that, given the ruling traditions, the grotesque and wasteful nuclear arms race was quite necessary, up to a point. Perhaps the safest course was to reach the point of mutual capacity for mutual destruction at the earliest possible moment, to put behind the days when "superiority" would offer a genuine military advantage. Certainly it can be counted a blessing that the nation which "stayed ahead" for as long as it counted for anything was the nation which by history and predilection would not launch a first strike.

Even as the arms race continued on its runaway course, a

mutual perception of mutual interest in national survival began to trace an alternative pattern for international behavior in the nuclear age. There was an intermittent counterpoint to the nuclear arms race.

Just before his death, Stalin apparently began to catch his first glimpse of the impact of atomic energy upon tradition and dogma; he is reported to have started backing away from the cardinal Marxist precept of the inevitability of wars between the socialist and capitalist camps. Several years later, Khrushchev declared that war was no longer inevitable owing, he said, to the great military power built up by the socialist side. In lieu of the old doctrine, Khrushchev postulated a so-called policy of peaceful coexistence. Peaceful coexistence, Khrushchev made plain, was but another way to conduct and extend the class struggle until the ultimate triumph of world Communism.

Yet the difference was a distinction between the prospect of total war and, at worst, limited wars by proxy or in "national liberation struggles." It was at least a thin wedge into the assumption of pervasive permanent conflict, an implicit admission that all national interests do not necessarily conflict, that some area of common interest does exist even between sovereign great powers.

By 1968, the United States and the Soviet Union were engaged in cooperative scientific research in a disarmed Antarctica. They had worked out principles to guide a continuing arms control and disarmament conference in Geneva; negotiated a treaty banning tests of nuclear weapons in the atmosphere, in outer space, and at sea; outlawed the orbiting of weapons of mass destruction in outer space; and negotiated a treaty intended to curb the spread of nuclear weapons. The next year the Super powers negotiated a draft treaty extending arms controls to the seabeds and ocean floors.

There were some signs, too, that the arms race was not irrevocably in a runaway state. In the United States, some advanced weapons systems were carried through the research and development stages and then rejected for production. The action-reaction dynamic was still strong but no longer quite so automatic. After breaking the moratorium, the Soviets carried out two series of atmospheric tests; the United States followed with only one. The Soviet decision to start deploying an antiballistic missile system led to a long debate, in and out of government, as to how the United States should react, or whether it should react at all.

Outside of the armaments field new technologies were making international agreement and cooperation an increasingly imperative axiom of modern life — for aerial navigation, the allocation of radio frequencies, weather reporting and forecasting, space law, and a lengthening list of activities which can only be regulated on a global basis. The areas of common interest were expanding a bit and the grip of pre-atomic tradition seemed to loosen a little.

The forces of political change began to work, too, within Communist societies.

Pluralism raised its subversive head in the Communist world; a faintly fresh breeze stirred tentatively in Russia. In Western Europe, by the mid-sixties, there were high hopes that détente had replaced the tensions of cold war. East-West contacts were on the rise; President Johnson offered to help "build bridges" between the two camps; and NATO turned to promoting relaxation of tensions as the first stage of a long journey toward arms control and ultimate East-West reconciliation. By mid-1968 Professor Sakharov, father of the Soviet H-bomb, was circulating to friends a breathtaking paper advocating Soviet-American reconciliation followed by world government and a universally open society on the grounds that "only in the free give-and-take of democratic life can science flourish." Shades of Niels Bohr!

At last it began to appear that the great confrontation in the center of Europe, where war was ended but no peace made, was dissolving — that Western firmness had bought time for the forces of change to begin to flow irreversibly in the Communist world. In the spring and summer of 1968, freshets of reform converged into a flood tide in Prague; but the yen for "socialism with a human face" and for open contacts with the outside world were on collision course with dogma, reaction, tradition, and passion for the status quo. In Moscow it looked as though things had gotten out of hand.

On the night of August 20-21, when the Soviet tanks rolled across the borders, the clock was again set back, not just in Prague but throughout the Soviet hegemony and in Russia too. In 1968 "bridge building" still looked like "neo-colonial imperialism" to the men in the Kremlin. The system itself, as Oppenheimer had said in his War College lecture of 1947, was in "very gross conflict" with openness and cooperation and community.

The Soviet invasion of Czechoslovakia in 1968 did more than postpone political change in the Soviet world. In early 1967 President Johnson had invited the Soviets to discuss the possibility of an agreement to limit inventories of strategic weapons on the two sides. He accepted the Soviet suggestion that defensive as well as offensive weapons should be included in any such talks. After repeated nudging, the Soviets at last agreed to engage in talks, a development which was to have been announced on August 21, 1968. The announcement was not made; the Soviets had invaded Czechoslovakia the night before. It would be late in November of 1969 before the first preliminary meeting was held.

While the project was still in abeyance, President Nixon was elected and inaugurated. He pronounced in favor of trying to negotiate a limitation on strategic arms; he began to speak of a "sufficiency" of nuclear weapons, an alternative and perhaps a more viable concept than "parity."

In the United States, at this time, men still counted numbers of weapons, multiplied them by "yields," and marshaled other statistics to show that the United States was still ahead or that the Soviet Union was about to "pull into the lead." Preparations for the arms talks proceeded cautiously on both sides; conventions that flowed from the preatomic military-political tradition were far from dead.

In the Soviet Union, the return toward orthodoxy did not seem to augur well for a radical break with received wisdom; since Czechsolovakia the ultraconservative school of power politics seemed decisive in Soviet decision-making.

Oppenheimer had noted in the course of his hearing that it was difficult to negotiate with the Russians about anything, that any instruments for the control of armaments were peculiarly difficult to design, and that when the two problems were put together "it was just the bleakest picture in the world."

Yet in merely agreeing to talk about the possibility of a

limitation of strategic weapons, the Soviets might be implying that a quantitative superiority over the United States
was beyond their reach, or that it was no longer worth seeking, or that some form of "parity" had been reached that
might be acceptable to them. At the same time, the formulation of a concept of nuclear "sufficiency" represented a
sharp and possibly decisive breakaway from past tradition.

Indeed the simple decision to talk at all might reach to the
roots of controlling conventions in international relations.
Despite the vast energies devoted to competition in nuclear arms, the major powers had behaved in practice as
though they believed it was even more important not to destroy each other than to obtain the capacity to do so. Now,
by agreeing to talks on the limitation of nuclear arms, they
implicitly called into question the basic motivations which
had generated the arms race and guaranteed its dynamic for
more than two decades: the quest for "security" through
"superiority."

Meanwhile the nuclear competition had reached yet another fork in the road. With the advent of antiballistic missile systems and the prospect of countervailing systems of
offensive weapons with multiple warheads, things had come
full circle. The way was open again for another try at agreement to forgo another multi-billion-dollar round which
would add to the sophistication of weapons technology but
leave the competitors more or less in the same relative position. It was reminiscent of the escalation from A-bombs to
H-bombs; yet an escalation to ABMs and MIRVs would
threaten the stability of the *pax atomica.*

Niels Bohr might well have insisted once more that it
must be easier to reach an agreement not to go into produc-

tion and deployment of untested new weaponry than to reduce weapons already in the arsenals; David Lilienthal might
well have looked upon ABMs and MIRVs as "pure gadgetry";
Dr. Bush might well have thought that a major effort should
be made to reach at least "a simple agreement" not to test the
next generation of weapons; and Dr. Conant might well have
felt that he was again seeing "an old movie and a punk one."
The basic dilemma that led to the formulation and the rejection of the Baruch Plan, to the reluctant passage from the
nuclear to the thermonuclear age, to the moratorium and
resumption of atmospheric testing was still with the world
as it entered the 1970s: the old political-military tradition
could not absorb the nuclear revolution.

Back in 1947 Oppenheimer said, "In order to work well,
people have to have some sense of participation in policy
making; in order to make policy they have to know things;
and in order to know things you have to tell them, you have
to let them learn."

In 1953 he said, "We do not operate well when the important facts . . . are known in secrecy and fear only to a
few men."

Several years after his death, Oppenheimer's compelling
faith in the potential of open society was at last put to a tough
test. Debate about the nuclear facts of life no longer was
confined to tight circles of officials, scientists, and military
professionals. For the first time since the advent of the
atomic age, nuclear weapon decisions were exposed to the
give-and-take of the open forum. As in other matters under
public debate, motives were mixed and the quality of dis-

course left something to be desired; but it was a long step
away from the dreary old exchanges of militray clichés and
pacifist slogans. Where Oppenheimer had failed in Operation Candor, others succeeded about a decade and a half later. In 1969 the United States Senate debated for a month
about ABMs and the public was learning about MIRVs.

The public was being exposed, as well, to concepts that
flew in the face of the inherited traditions.

In the April 1969 issue of the *Bulletin of the Atomic Scientists,* George W. Rathjens spoke of "the qualitatively stable
'balance of terror.'"

In the August issue of the same magazine, Herbert F. York,
director of defense research and engineering in the Eisenhower administration, examined the numbers and charac-
teristics of strategic weapons available for delivery from both
sides by missiles, bombers, and submarines; and he concluded
that "what all these complicated details add up to can be expressed in a single word: parity." York went on: "This is
clearly not numerical equality in the number of warheads or
in the number of megatons or in the total 'throw weight';
in fact . . . simultaneous equality in these three figures is
entirely impossible. It is, rather, parity with respect to strategic objectives . . .

". . . In short we now have parity in the only sense that
counts."

This led York to express some hope for the outcome of
SALT. The time, he wrote, is propitious: ". . . both sides
will be discussing the matter from a position of parity. Moreover, this parity seems reasonably stable and likely to endure
for several years."

York, however, had another point to make: a technological

approach to strategic thinking "leads to a completely hopeless situation . . . Unless the arms race is stopped by political action outside the two [United States and Soviet] defense establishments, I feel reasonably sure there will be another 'crash program' response . . ."

McGeorge Bundy read the York argument on substituting political for technological decisions and agreed. "I find this conclusion compelling," he wrote in the October issue of *Foreign Affairs*.

In the same magazine in which Oppenheimer's heresy first came to light, McGeorge Bundy, sixteen years later, wrote:

> The next year or two offers the United States and the Soviet Union what may be the best chance yet to limit their extravagant contest in strategic weapons. We Americans may not understand this opportunity very well, and our friends in Russia may not understand it either. That weakness of understanding, together with the transcendent importance of the subject, is an excuse for one more effort to put some light on it . . .

Bundy then proceeded to put considerable light on the subject. A credible nuclear deterrent, Bundy said, is still necessary: ". . . It seems to me wholly plain that a credible strategic nuclear deterrent is indispensable to the peace . . . We have bought and paid for parity and we must not lose it . . ."

On the other hand, said Bundy: ". . . The object of political men — quite rightly — is that these weapons should never be used . . . Political leaders, whether here or in Russia, . . . see cities and people as part of what they are trying to help — not as targets. They live with the daily struggle to make a little progress — to build things — to grow things — to lift the quality of life a little . . . And that is why the deterrent does work."

But the day is long past, Bundy said, when it makes any sense to carry on the race:

> The neglected truth about the present strategic arms race . . . is that in terms of international political behavior that race has now become almost completely irrelevant. The new weapons systems which are being developed by each of the two great powers will provide neither protection nor opportunity in any serious political sense. Politically the strategic nuclear arms race is in a stalemate . . .
>
> In light of the certain prospect of retaliation there has been literally no chance at all that any sane political authority, in either the United States or the Soviet Union, would consciously choose to start a nuclear war. This proposition is true for the past, the present and the foreseeable future. For sane men on both sides the balance of terror is overwhelmingly persuasive . . .

Indeed, said Bundy, the whole idea of straining for superiority in strategic nuclear weapons has become a myth:

> . . . The basic consequence of considering this matter politically and not technically is the conclusion that beyond a point long since passed the escalation of the strategic nuclear race makes no sense for either the Soviet Union or the United States . . . in political, as distinct from technical, terms we have all been wrong to talk of nuclear superiority . . . Sufficiency is what we both have now, in ample measure, and no superiority worth having can be achieved . . . A stalemate is a stalemate either way around.
>
> . . . each great power must move from a zealous concern for his own advantage to a sober acceptance of parity.

There is "an enormous gulf," Bundy wrote, "between what political leaders really think about nuclear weapons and what is assumed in complex calculations of relative 'advantage' in simulated strategic warfare." The difficulty is, he went on, that while political leaders in both countries "may not themselves be persuaded by the refined calculations of the nuclear gamesmen," they at the same time "do not find it prudent to expose them for the political irrelevance they are."

The result, Bundy wrote, is this: "The current race has become a wildly irrelevant technical competition which brings no help to statesmen and sooner or later the true statesman must say so." He seemed to be arguing for something like Operation Candor.

Yet Bundy did not put the final blame on political leaders. He reviewed the Senate debate on the ABM issue and found that "the internal politics of the strategic arms race has remained the prisoner of its technology . . . those who oppose the ABM tend to argue that it might not work technically — not that it is irrelevant politically." Then he said: ". . . I know of no escape from the conclusion that both in his sensible abhorrence of nuclear conflict and his persistent attachment to still more weapons systems the political leader is reflecting his constituency. The fault is less in our leaders than in ourselves."

A "continuous course of unilateral strategic disarmament" was out of the question for Bundy. "It will take two," he wrote, "to cap the volcano of strategic competition." Yet in the end the best hope seemed to him to reside in the open society and the open forum: ". . . We are still 'ahead' and we may also be closer to a national recognition that such a lead means nothing. Our process of government does not impose a requirement of fear and suspicion that is remotely like that imposed by the Soviet party apparatus. We now have a fully developed public debate which will not die down . . .

"I believe that the American people know in their bones that nuclear weapons are different . . ."

Bundy, of course, was addressing the predicament that Oppenheimer prophesied by projecting the "tough fix" of 1953 into the next decade; and he came out where Oppenheimer did, on the side of public discussion of "the nuclear facts of life" so long held "in secrecy and in fear" by a handful of men.

At long last Oppenheimer's heresy had become respectable — perhaps well on its way toward becoming the conventional wisdom of tomorrow. It was no longer a punishable offense to say out loud, as Bundy did, that the time had arrived when it "means nothing" to be "ahead" in strategic nuclear armaments.

Because he understood the deep resistance to change in closed societies, Oppenheimer was an early pessimist about the possibility of reaching agreement with the Soviet Union for controlling atomic energy.

Yet to the end he could have gone on describing himself as a "dedicated optimist." For Einstein and Lord Russell and Professor Sakharov and many other scientists, it was impossible intellectually to conceive of safety in the atomic age without world government.

Oppenheimer worried greatly about the possibility of nuclear war, but he never believed that the only alternatives in the nuclear age were instant utopia or sudden disaster. He sensed that between the quick and the dead lies the real world in which fumbling societies somehow absorb scientific revolutions into the body politic and bumbling men somehow get the message from the handwriting on the wall.

Oppenheimer suspected that short of a "government of the whole" lay a pluralistic if patchwork world society held together if not by law, then by a perceived community of interests. As he put it in the last of his Reith lectures on "Science and the Common Understanding":

It is a cruel and humorless sort of pun that so powerful a present form of tyranny should call itself by the very name of a belief in community, by a word "communism" which in other times evoked memories of villages and village inns and of artisans concerting their skills, and of men of learning content with anonymity. But perhaps only a malignant end can follow the systematic belief that all communities are one community; that all truth is one truth; that all experience is compatible with all other; that total knowledge is possible; that all that is potential can exist as actual. This is not man's fate; this is not his path; to force him on it makes him resemble not that divine image of the all-knowing and all-powerful but the helpless, iron-bound prisoner of a dying world. The open society, the unrestricted access to knowledge, the unplanned and uninhibited association of men for its furtherance — these are what may make a vast, complex, ever-growing, ever-changing, ever more specialized and expert technological world nevertheless a world of human community.

Oppenheimer's lectures over BBC were in 1953. Sixteen years later, as the nuclear giants approached strategic arms limitation, the closed and open societies were still in gross conflict as political systems. Yet a new question seemed to be

taking shape: Could deep political change in international behavior occur, after all, without creating a world government
or even a world of open societies?

Beyond that lay the question of when, or whether, in the
field of political action, men would learn "to throw away
those instruments of action and those modes of description
which are not appropriate to the reality we are trying to
discern."

Notes

Bibliography

Index

Notes

INTRODUCTION

1. *In the Matter of J. Robert Oppenheimer — Transcript of Hearing Before Personnel Security Board* (Washington, D.C.: Government Printing Office, 1954) (hereafter cited as *Transcript*); *In the Matter of J. Robert Oppenheimer — Texts of Principal Documents and Letters* (Washington, D.C.: Government Printing Office, 1954). *Note:* Both of these publications are out of print and difficult to find.
2. Joseph and Stewart Alsop, *We Accuse* (New York: Simon & Schuster Inc., 1954), p. 1.

CHAPTER 1

1. An extensive description of life at Göttingen is found in *Brighter Than a Thousand Suns* by Robert Jungk (New York: Grove Press, 1958).
2. *Bulletin of the Atomic Scientists,* October 1967.

CHAPTER 2

1. *Bulletin of the Atomic Scientists,* October 1967.
2. Haakon Chevalier, *Oppenheimer: The Story of a Friendship* (New York: George Braziller, 1965).
3. *Transcript,* p. 581.
4. *Transcript,* p. 322.

5. *Transcript,* p. 644.
6. *Transcript,* p. 577.

CHAPTER 3

1. Laura Fermi, the widow of Enrico Fermi, has written a detailed account of the amazing flight of scientists, artists, writers, and professional people from Europe to the United States in *Illustrious Immigrants* (Chicago: University of Chicago Press, 1968).
2. The fullest popular account of work at Los Alamos is in *Day of Trinity,* by Lansing Lamont (New York: Atheneum, 1965); *Brighter Than a Thousand Suns* also has extensive material.
3. Hans Bethe, *Bulletin of the Atomic Scientists,* October, 1967.
4. *Transcript,* p. 170.
5. Ibid., pp. 649, 653.
6. Ibid., p. 264.
7. Ibid., p. 167.
8. Two books, taken together, provide the relevant documentation of the U.S. decision to bomb Hiroshima and Nagasaki and the consequent surrender by Japan. They are *On Active Service in Peace and War,* by Henry L. Stimson and McGeorge Bundy (New York: Harper & Brothers, 1948) and *Japan's Decision to Surrender,* by Robert J. C. Butow (Stanford University Press, 1967).

CHAPTER 4

1. This and other quotations from Bohr are excerpted from his memorandum to President Roosevelt of July 1944 as published at Appendix A to *Brighter Than a Thousand Suns.*
2. From an article "Niels Bohr and the Making of The Bomb," by J. Robert Oppenheimer in the *New York Review of Books,* December 17, 1964.
3. The so-called Franck Report is published as Appendix B to *Brighter Than a Thousand Suns.*

CHAPTER 5

1. This and subsequent quotations in this chapter attributed to Mr. Lilienthal are excerpted from David E. Lilienthal, *Journals,* 3 vols. (New York: Harper & Row, 1964), Vol. 2.

2. *A Report on the International Control of Atomic Energy,* March 16, 1946, Department of State Publication 2498, U.S. Government Printing Office.
3. Alexander Werth, Moscow correspondent of *The Saturday Times* of London, September 24, 1945.
4. Speech at a meeting in the Stalin Electoral Area of Moscow, February 9, 1946.
5. A Report on the International Control of Atomic Energy.
6. Ibid.

CHAPTER 6

1. This and other quotations and accounts of the proceedings of the United Nations Atomic Energy Commission have been taken from the UN's verbatim record.
2. Quotations from, and descriptions of, the U.S. proposals have been drawn from *A Report on the International Control of Atomic Energy,* prepared for the Secretary of State's Committee on Atomic Energy, March 26, 1946, Department of State Publication 2498; and *Atomic Energy — Growth of a Policy,* Department of State Publication 2702.
3. Members of the United Nation's Atomic Energy Commission were Great Britain, France, China, the United Kingdom, the United States, Canada, Brazil, Mexico, Poland, Egypt, the Netherlands, and Australia.

CHAPTER 7

1. *Transcript,* p. 40.
2. Ibid., p. 322.
3. Ibid., p. 344.
4. Ibid., p. 42.

CHAPTER 8

1. J. Robert Oppenheimer, "Nuclear Energy and American Foreign Policy," *Foreign Affairs Quarterly,* July 1953.
2. Ralph Lapp, *The New Priesthood* (New York: Harper & Row, 1965).
3. Quotations in the rest of this chapter, if not otherwise identified, have been excerpted from a collection of addresses published under the title *The Open Mind,* by J. Robert Oppenheimer (New York: Simon & Schuster, 1955).

CHAPTER 9

1. *Transcript,* p. 46.
2. Ibid., p. 684.
3. Walter Millis, *Arms and the State* (New York: The Twentieth Century Fund, 1958) p. 240.
4. As quoted by Millis in *Arms and the State,* p. 248.
5. Ibid., pp. 248-249.
6. *Transcript,* p. 497 ff.
7. Ibid., p. 396.
8. Ibid., pp. 497-498.
8. Ibid., p. 684.

CHAPTER 10

1. *Lilienthal Journals,* Vol. 2, p. 570.
2. *Transcript,* p. 658 ff.
3. Ibid., p. 460.
4. *Lilienthal Journals,* Vol. 2., p. 582.
5. Lewis L. Strauss, *Men and Decisions* (Garden City, N.Y.: Doubleday & Company, 1962) pp. 216-17.
6. *Transcript,* p. 716.
7. Ibid., p. 461.
8. Ibid., p. 395.
9. Ibid., p. 510.
10. Ibid., p. 519.
11. Ibid., p. 605.
12. Ibid., p. 235-236.
13. Ibid., p. 453.
14. Ibid., p. 513.
15. Ibid., p. 605.
16. Ibid., p. 563 ff.
17. Ibid., p. 328.
18. Ibid., p. 359 ff.
19. Ibid., p. 647 ff.
20. Ibid., p. 329.
21. Ibid., p. 455.
22. Ibid., p. 510.
23. Ibid., p. 518-519.

24. Ibid., p. 79.
25. Ibid., p. 80.
26. Ibid., pp. 79-80.
27. *Lilienthal Journals,* Vol. 2, p. 580.

CHAPTER 11

1. *Lilienthal Journals,* Vol. 2, p. 582.
2. Ibid., pp. 584-585.
3. Ibid., p. 591.
4. Ibid., p. 584.
5. Ibid., p. 615.
6. *Men and Decisions,* p. 223.
7. Ibid., pp. 219-222.
8. Ibid., Appendix, p. 440.
9. *Lilienthal Journals,* p. 632.
10. Ibid., p. 633.
11. *Transcript,* p. 329.
12. Ibid., p. 80.
13. From radio broadcast of February 12, 1950, as quoted on p. 962 of the *Transcript.*

CHAPTER 12

1. *Transcript,* p. 642.
2. Walter Millis, *Arms and the State* (New York: The Twentieth Century Fund, 1958); p. 256.
3. *Transcript,* p. 86.
4. Ibid., p. 83.
5. Ibid., p. 73.
6. Maxwell D. Taylor, *The Uncertain Trumpet* (New York: Harper & Brothers, 1960); pp. 15-16.
7. *Transcript,* p. 83.
8. Ibid., p. 787.
9. Ibid., p. 46.
10. Ibid., p. 58.
11. Ibid., p. 94.
12. Ibid., p. 720.
13. Ibid., p. 720.

14. Ibid., p. 305.
15. Ibid., p. 953.
16. Ibid., p. 747.
17. Ibid., pp. 762-763.
18. Ibid., p. 759.
19. Ibid., p. 584.
20. Robert S. McNamara, *The Essence of Security* (New York: Harper & Row, 1968).
21. *Transcript,* p. 768.
22. Ibid., p. 85.
23. Ibid., pp. 526-527.
24. Ibid., p. 85.
25. Ibid., p. 457.
26. Ibid., pp. 338-339.
27. Ibid., p. 339.
28. Ibid., p. 457.
29. Ibid., p. 726.
30. Ibid., p. 598.
31. Ibid., p. 952.
32. Ibid., p. 923.
33. Ibid., p. 925.
34. Ibid., p. 924.
35. Ibid., pp. 952-953.
36. Quotations attributed to Griggs in the remainder of this chapter are scattered through his testimony, which appears on pp. 742-770 of the *Transcript.*
37. *Transcript,* p. 941.
38. Ibid., p. 938.
39. Ibid., pp. 926-932.
40. Ibid., pp. 757-758.
41. Ibid., p. 748.
42. Ibid., p. 600.
43. Ibid., p. 96.
44. Ibid., p. 461.
45. Ibid., p. 496.
46. Ibid., pp. 517-518.
47. Ibid., p. 95.
48. Ibid., p. 97.
49. Ibid., p. 97.

CHAPTER 13

1. *Transcript,* p. 562.
2. Emmet John Hughes, *The Ordeal of Power* (New York: Atheneum, 1963), p. 72.
3. *The Uncertain Trumpet,* p. 17.
4. *Transcript,* p. 95.
5. Ibid., p. 96.
6. Robert Donovan, *Eisenhower: The Inside Story* (New York: Harper & Row, 1956). pp. 184-185.
7. *Transcript,* pp. 93-94.
8. *The Uncertain Trumpet,* p. 110.
9. Ibid., p. 121.
10. Ibid., p. 108.

CHAPTER 14

1. *Transcript,* p. 734.
2. Ibid., p. 357.
3. This and additional quotations in this chapter are from "Atomic Energy and American Foreign Policy," J. Robert Oppenheimer, *Foreign Affairs Quarterly,* July 1953.

CHAPTER 15

1. *Transcript,* p. 734.
2. This and all further quotations in this chapter are from "The Hidden Struggle for the H-Bomb," *Fortune,* May 1953.

CHAPTER 16

1. *Transcript,* p. 468.
2. Ibid., p. 499.
3. Ibid., p. 94.
4. Ibid., p. 94.
5. *In the Matter of J. Robert Oppenheimer:* Texts of Principal Documents and Letters of Personnel Security Board / General Manager / Commissioners (Washington: United States Government Printing Office, 1954), pp. 13-14.

6. Ibid., p. 56.
7. Haakon Chevalier, *Oppenheimer: The Story of a Friendship* (New York: George Braziller, 1965), p. 206.
8. *Transcript,* p. 838.
9. *Men and Decisions,* pp. 267-268.
10. Ibid.
11. Letter from R. D. Nichols to J. Robert Oppenheimer, December 23, 1953; *Transcript,* pp. 3-7.
12. *Men and Decisions,* Appendix, pp. 443-445.
13. *Men and Decisions,* p. 277.
14. *Transcript,* p. 22.

CHAPTER 17

1. *Transcript,* pp. 269-270.
2. Ibid., p. 735.
3. Ibid., p. 736.
4. Ibid., pp. 565-567.

CHAPTER 18

1. *Transcript,* p. 680.
2. Ibid., p. 702.
3. Ibid., p. 709.
4. Ibid., p. 772.
5. Ibid., p. 743.
6. Ibid., p. 694.
7. Ibid., p. 684.
8. Ibid., p. 746.
9. Ibid., p. 751.
10. Ibid., p. 753.
11. Ibid., p. 756.
12. Ibid., p. 727.
13. Ibid., p. 710.
14. Ibid., p. 720.
15. Ibid., p. 702.
16. Ibid., p. 684.
17. Ibid., p. 684.
18. Ibid., p. 685.

19. Ibid., p. 685.
20. Ibid., p. 724.
21. Ibid., p. 782.
22. Ibid., p. 784.
23. Ibid., p. 788.
24. Ibid., p. 706.
25. Ibid., p. 660.
26. Ibid., p. 663.
27. Ibid., p. 660.
28. Ibid., p. 664.
29. Ibid., p. 663.
30. Ibid., p. 664.
31. Ibid., pp. 660-661, 669.
32. Ibid., p. 666.
33. Ibid., p. 750.
34. Ibid., p. 704.
35. Ibid., p. 702.
36. Ibid., p. 709.
37. Ibid., p. 710.
38. Ibid., p. 726.

CHAPTER 19

1. This and other quotations from the Gray Report and the "findings" of the general manager and commissioners of the AEC are from *In the Matter of J. Robert Oppenheimer:* Texts of Principal Documents and Letters of Personnel Security Board, General Manager, Commissioners. United States Government Printing Office, 1954.

CHAPTER 20

1. Press dispatches from London, March 3, 1955.

CHAPTER 21

1. J. Robert Oppenheimer, *Science and the Common Understanding* (New York: Simon & Schuster, 1953).

Bibliography

Alsop, Joseph and Stewart. *We Accuse! The Story of the Miscarriage of American Justice in the Case of J. Robert Oppenheimer.* New York: Simon & Schuster, Inc., 1954.

Borden, William Liscum. *There Will Be No Time: The Revolution in Strategy.* New York: The MacMillan Company, 1946.

Butow, Robert J. C. *Japan's Decision to Surrender.* Stanford: Stanford University Press, 1967.

Chevalier, Haakon. *Oppenheimer: The Story of a Friendship.* New York: George Braziller, 1965.

Compton, Arthur H. *Atomic Quest.* New York: Oxford University Press, 1956.

Davis, Nuel Pharr. *Lawrence and Oppenheimer.* New York: Simon & Schuster, Inc., 1968.

Department of State. *Growth of a Policy: The International Control of Atomic Energy.* (An Informal Summary Record of the Official Declarations and Proposals Relating to the International Control of Atomic Energy Made between April 6, 1945, and October 15, 1946.) Washington, D.C.: The United States Government Printing Office, 1945-46.

Fermi, Laura. *Illustrious Immigrants: The Intellectual Migration from Europe, 1930-41.* Chicago: University of Chicago Press, 1968.

Gilpin, Robert. *American Scientists and Nuclear Weapons Policy.* Princeton: Princeton University Press, 1968.

Groves, Leslie R. *Now It Can Be Told: The Story of the Manhattan Project.* New York: Harper & Row, 1962.

Hughes, Emmet John. *The Ordeal of Power: A Political Memoir of the Eisenhower Years.* New York: Atheneum, 1963.

In the Matter of J. Robert Oppenheimer: Transcript of Hearing before Personnel Security Board. Washington, D.C.: The United States Government Printing Office, 1954.

Jungk, Robert. *Brighter Than a Thousand Suns: The Story of the Men Who Made the Bomb.* New York: Grove Press, Inc., 1958.

Lamont, Lansing. *Day of Trinity.* New York: Atheneum, 1965.

Lang, Daniel. *An Inquiry into Enoughness: Of Bombs and Men and Staying Alive.* New York: McGraw-Hill Book Company, 1965.

Lapp, Ralph. *Atoms and People.* New York: Harper & Brothers, 1956.

———. *Kill and Overkill.* New York: Basic Books, 1962.

———. *The New Force: The Story of Atoms and People.* New York: Harper & Brothers, 1953.

———. *The New Priesthood: The Scientific Elite and the Uses of Power.* New York: Harper & Row, 1965.

Lilienthal, David E. *Journals.* Vol. 2. New York: Harper & Row, 1964.

McNamara, Robert S. *The Essence of Security: Reflections in Office.* New York: Harper & Row, 1968.

Millis, Walter; Mansfield, Harvey C.; and Stein, Harold. *Arms and the State.* New York: The Twentieth Century Fund, 1958.

Millis, Walter, and Duffield, E. S., eds. *The Forrestal Diaries.* New York: The Viking Press, 1951.

Oppenheimer, J. Robert. *Science and the Common Understanding.* New York: Simon & Schuster, Inc., 1953.

———. *The Flying Trapeze: Three Crises for Physicists.* New York: Oxford University Press, 1964.

———. *The Open Mind.* New York: Simon & Schuster, Inc., 1955.

Personal Security Board [AEC] General Manager, [AEC] Commissioners. *In the Matter of J. Robert Oppenheimer: Texts of Principal Documents and Letters of Personnel Security Board.* Washington, D.C.: The United States Government Printing Office, 1954.

Ratnjens, George W. *The Future of the Strategic Arms Race: Options for the 1970's.* New York: Carnegie Endowment for International Peace, 1969.

Rouzé, Nichel. *Robert Oppenheimer: The Man and His Theories.* New York: Paul S. Eriksson, Inc., 1965.

Smyth, Henry de Wolf. *Atomic Energy for Military Purposes.* Princeton: Princeton University Press, 1945.

Stern, Philip M. *The Oppenheimer Case: Security on Trial.* New York: Harper & Row, 1969.

Stimson, Henry L., and Bundy, McGeorge. *On Active Service in Peace and War.* New York: Harper & Brothers, 1948.

Strauss, Lewis L. *Men and Decisions.* Garden City, N.Y.: Doubleday & Company, Inc., 1962.

Taylor, Maxwell D. *The Uncertain Trumpet.* New York: Harper & Brothers, 1960.

Truman, Harry S. *Memoirs.* 2 vols. Garden City, N.Y.: Doubleday & Company, Inc., 1958.

Tugwell, Rexford G. *A Chronicle of Jeopardy* 1945-1955. Chicago: University of Chicago Press, 1956.

Vandenberg, Arthur H., Jr., and Morris, Joe Alex, eds. *The Private Papers of Senator Vandenberg.* Boston: Houghton Mifflin Company, 1952.

Index

3-4-71

DATE DUE

New Books	APR 15 71		

GAYLORD | | | PRINTED IN U.S A